The Myth
of
Mediation Neutrality

also by Kevin Boileau

Theory

Genuine Reciprocity and Group Authenticity
(First Edition)

Genuine Reciprocity and Group Authenticity:
(The Social Ontology of Sartre & Foucault)

The Algebra of History
(with David A. Boileau)

Essays on Phenomenology and the Self

Manifesto on Solidarity; Ethics for a New World

Coming Soon

Phenomenology
& Mediation

Critical Existential
Psycho-Analysis

Workbook for Psychoanalysis
& Mediation

Literary

The Patient

The Blue Pearl

Abject Poverty

99 Deceptions

The Separation

The Return

The Outlaw Series Vol. 1

Make Me Stay

Sexxual Lies

A Turtle's Murder

Coming Soon

Northside

The Bishop... A Fisherman

3 Rivers

Sweet Monogamy

Boileau Conflict Solutions

BCS Dispute Resolution is an imprint of EPIS Press dedicated to producing useful and informative texts in mediation, negotiation, and dispute resolution design. Based on research in phenomenology, psychoanalysis, critical theory, and game theory mathematics, the books that we produce present innovative theory and practice to teachers, scholars, and professionals in the fields of dispute resolution, including mediators, lawyers, negotiators, psychologists, collaborative facilitators, life coaches, and specialized family lenders/Realtors.

For more information:
solutionsbcs@gmail.com
www.boileaucs.com
www.bcsmediationtraining.com

EPIS Press
31 Fort Missoula Road, Suite 4
Missoula, MT 59804 USA
epispublishing1@gmail.com

Printed in the United States of America
First Edition July 2014

Library of Congress Cataloging-in-Publication Data
1. psychoanalysis 2. applied psychoanalysis 3. mediation
4. applied phenomenology 5. conflict resolution 6. title

Cover Design: Tia Hopkins
Author Photo: NTG
Author Seal: Adrian Balasa

ISBN 978-0-9899301-9-2

The Myth
of
Mediation Neutrality

The Psychoanalytic, Phenomenological, and
Linguistic-Structural Approach
to Mediation

Dr. Kevin Boileau
Ph.D., J.D., LL.M.

Basis of the Text

The prolegomena that follows comes about from several thousand clinical hours conducting relational psychotherapy, group therapy, and mediation. It comes from thinking and writing about the application of phenomenology and psychoanalysis to the important work of cooperative conflict resolution. It is the first book in a series of new thoughts and suggestions about how to develop mediation practice from a foundation of deep psychoanalytic, social, linguistic, and ontological theory.

The book is preparatory, which means that much of it is primitive and that it, therefore, must be worked out with further research, thinking, and practice. It is the first book in a series that will include additional theoretical perspectives, including game theory, non-verbal communication, inter-cultural communication, gender studies, ethnicity studies, linguistic and discourse studies, and much more. It is our attempt to reframe much of the discussion in mediation theory that stems from an outmoded philosophy of mind and a new philosophical anthropology of humans that must be created: this also leads to exciting new thought regarding the conceptual openings that we can create through phenomenological and psychoanalytic methods.

I have been in the favorable position to have backgrounds both in law and in psychoanalysis; as such, my professional practice has been formerly drawn into two divergent directions until the data in my clinical practice suggested that psychoanalytic knowledge and methodology has something of value to offer mediation practice. Then these directions integrated. Over and over again, in all of my professional practice and experience watching and teaching, I have learned how much we focus on the phenomenon in front of us and then treat it as an objective problem to solve. Philosophically and dynamically, the focus is on the object (the mediation process/protocol and its parties) and not enough on the subject (the mediator herself); there is even less focus on the process between the mediator and the parties. Thus, even if a well-trained mediator applies established mediation techniques and is experienced in them, the success of the process can suffer to the extent that the mediator is unaware of the unconscious (or less-than-conscious) dynamics that may occur without his or her knowledge.

This book addresses that problem in a preliminary way, which is why I think about it as a prolegomena—an introduction of sorts—the purpose of which is to motivate us to think about the effects of unconscious forces that originate in us, the professional mediators. I have received mixed reactions about this sort of thinking: Some practitioners welcome the insight they may gain from considering this new dimension; others feel anxious about what they may discover. Likewise, some "purist" analysts believe that psychoanalysis cannot be legitimately used in these new "applied" ways; others are open. It remains to be seen, but I do have a strong intuition—and propose it as a scientific and pragmatic hypothesis—that there may be valuable insight we can learn from opening up a psychoanalytic dimension in mediation. Freud himself believed that we could extend the practice to education and, I believe by implication, to other practices and forums. As such, my prolegomena is humble in scope, preliminary in its coverage, and tentative in its conclusions. It comes from my own experience that—as we know—must always be tested by considering the "unknowable" unconscious, along with the dialectically corrective set of theoretical tools we construct. With these thoughts in mind, I now to proceed to delineate the problem, work out the theory, and suggest the beginning of a new praxis for mediation practitioners.

I apologize for all mistakes and errors, lacunae, and short sightedness. However, I strongly assert the value of our research and this book. We are at an exciting historical crossroads, and I believe that the development of mediation practice and its underlying theory will have a positive impact on the way we en-frame difference and resolve interpersonal conflict. The work we do today will have lasting effects decades if not centuries from now. I have intentionally kept the number of endnotes and references to a minimum, erring on the side of ease of reading and general approach. Every one of the concepts I address is carefully explicated in other texts, and I have provided a clear pathway for further research.

Prof. Kevin Boileau
Winter, 2014
Writing from Missoula, Montana USA
BCS Dispute Resolution Institute
EPIS Psychoanalytic Research Institute
Center for Global Advanced Studies
Global Solidarity Foundation

Contents

I:
Introduction
to the Problem

The traditional view is that a mediator is a neutral, third party who helps two or more conflicting parties cooperatively resolve their differences. The implication has always been that the mediator — as professional — makes judgments and decisions by analyzing the case before him in a dispassionate, uninvolved way. Interestingly enough, this belief is analogous to the Cartesian-Newtonian epistemological position that holds that one can be an independent observer of an objective world, in science or in daily life. More practically, this has also been the clinical view in most contemporary psychotherapy and psychoanalysis. (See my Essays on Phenomenology and the Self, Essay One).[1] However, I am skeptical about this position, both epistemologically and clinically. What remains an open question is whether a mediator can actually ever be a "neutral third." There are derivative questions, as well, including the implications for mediation practice in general, should we discover that the notion of neutrality is a convenient fiction, an ideological myth that covers deeper realities.[2]

Let us consider that the personality of the mediator — her moods, styles, communications, and non-verbal indicators — may actually influence the thoughts, feelings, and behaviors of the conflicting parties in a mediation encounter. Let us consider that these processes might be largely unconscious. If this is the case, then what appears to be happening in mediation, a so-called objective, neutral (and because of that, fair) process is not actually happening at all. In this case, the process is nothing more than Shakespearean theatre — a cipher with multiple interpretations and distortions.

A related problem involves the potential lack of knowledge of the mediator about the disputing parties. If the mediator has worked with both parties on an ongoing and long-term basis, the mediator could theoretically become aware of what is pervasive in each party's makeup, manifesting in a broad spectrum of relations; in combination with the mediator's own self awareness, this could potentially create a framework for an analytic process. Nevertheless, in many if not most mediation contexts, the mediator knows very little about the parties except for superficial information about the nature of the dispute and perhaps some facts about the parties themselves. This lack, in my judgment, prevents the sort of dialectical awareness that comes from an analytic framework from emerging. In that case, the mediator is left to his or her own intuitions which, as any analyst knows, are narcissistic in nature and which preclude a reasonable, fair, and analytic process—in various degrees depending upon the level of distortion.[3]

More particularly, what a disputing party chooses to speak of, or how she chooses to frame her position or needs—I believe—is partly influenced by the presence and behavior of the second/other disputant as well as the mediator.[4] If we substitute in a different mediator, we consequently substitute in a different range of characteristics and behavior. That is, quite different events, issues, moods, and self-problematics will emerge with different mediators. I take it as obvious that these variations of a disputant's self-structure (this notion, by the way, is postmodern in character and much anti-Cartesian) can affect at a crucial level the process that occurs. Without knowledge of these different self-structures and without the benefit of a resulting analytic framework, the process could be arbitrary even though it appears fair and neutral. Moreover, mediators who play the role of a neutral third party by engaging in the requisite behaviors actually influence the parties in ways of which they are unaware. Again, this results in a convenient ideology that serves no one.

The truth of the matter is that each disputing party reacts differently—in unconscious ways—to the (deceptive) role of a professional who tries to be an "independent and neutral" mediator.[5] What I propose is a new and different way of viewing mediation. Instead of the belief that a mediator can be neutral and can understand the conflicting parties objectively, I propose that the mediator cannot theoretically ever be neutral. In the alternative, we could interpret mediation as a situation involving the complex self-systems of all three (or more) participants, including the mediator—with both conscious and unconscious elements of all at play. In principle, this jeopardizes the regulative ideal of that neutrality and replaces it with a more complex system but one that more accurately describes and captures the phenomenon of mediation.[6]

In this weltanschauung the parties work together with the active participation of a mediator who is unable to be neutral for a number of reasons that can be explained psychoanalytically. I believe that what is required in its place is critical dialogue and, more seriously, a dialectic that allows us to engage these unconscious cyclical elements consciously. There is much work to do in developing a prolegomena to such an analytic, but it starts with a (Heideggarian) ontological focus and Hegelian dialectic—a critical discourse.[7] I will address these notions as well proceed into the methodology, keeping in mind that extensive research ought to be done on them in the future. What's important is my argument that if we acknowledge what is really going on in mediation (at a deep social-ontological level[8]), we can begin to develop theory and practice in such a way that will elevate its standards both practically and ethically.

Let us continue to explore a psychoanalytic approach. The classical analytic approach assumes an unconscious, and the existential phenomenological does not. (See my Essays on Phenomenology and the Self, Essay One). However, although they are radically different philosophies of mind on the surface, they both share the binary distinction between a) awareness and b) lack of awareness (albeit with different terms). They are also convergent in that they purport to identify and examine transcendent and immanent structures that affect self-construction and sociality.[9]

At the outset, I ask the reader to consider these different philosophies of mind, especially as they bear on professional practice differently. Perhaps we will see that each approach offers valuable insight into the orientation and methods of the practitioner in the professional encounter. The hope is to broaden and deepen perspective in order to enhance ethical and pragmatic sensibility. To this end, I have constructed, clinically and theoretically, two different psychoanalytic models, which I call "Model A," which is the existential psychoanalytic approach and "Model B," which is the classical psychoanalytic approach, in which there are three variations. There is also a rudimentary analysis of some of the considerations of a "Model C," which is the linguistic-structural approach. I will also present chapters on it.[10]

Let's first engage in a preparatory analysis by engaging in a deconstruction of the Cartesian position and its practical correlative, which assumes the possibility of a "neutral" third party in mediation— derivative isomorphic analyses follow in other, later segments (see Descartes' Meditations on First Philosophy).[11] Later, I will demonstrate how it is the powerful machinery of phenomenology that we will bring to bear on the problem of the detached, neutral observer of phenomena. The idea of a neutral observer is the modernist idea that in all scientific inquiry there is a radical split between subject and object. This assumption leads to the position that an impersonal observer could, with the right kind of methodology, discover the truth about the nature of reality, both natural and social. In contrast, however, the phenomenological approach holds that no subject "knower" can fairly exclude herself from the [objective?] phenomenon that he is perceiving and studying. In this position, there is no radical split between subject and object and therefore no way to ever obtain objective, detached truth about the nature of the universe. Instead, our goal would be to interrogate and understand the contents of the consciousness of the mediator, and the parties. In practice, it means to effects of the unconscious that we must excavate or illuminate.

For the phenomenologist, any knower [human investigator] is always already embedded in a complex of interrelationships with the natural, spiritual, social, and internal world. In short, the very act of inquiry affects the subject knower in ways that are difficult if not impossible to discern. Furthermore, investigative behavior has additional effects on the object of the investigation as well as on other subjects involved in the inquiry. Unfortunately, Descartes's test of "clearness and distinctness" fails under this sort of rigorous phenomenological reassessment of the foundations of scientific inquiry. (See a good history of philosophy such as The Routledge History of Philosophy for summary comments about modernism and Descartes's contributions to it.)

It is through the work of Brentano, Husserl, and Heidegger that we begin to disabuse ourselves of the Cartesian position by realizing that the arbitrary subject-object derivative is a distortion of our more primary being-in-the-world, which is a concept that tries to explain our complex, embedded nature. (See my Essays on Phenomenology and the

Self). Let us then focus on the nature of the problem again, at the risk of repetitiveness: The received view of mediation is that it can actually be a fair process if the mediator is neutral and certain structures and procedures are in place. Phenomenology suggests, in principle [and in part], that because the radical subject-object split is an illusion, the mediator cannot possibly ever truly be neutral. I am asserting more than the usual commentary about bias, prejudice, and the like. I am propounding that there is a deeper level—the ontological—at which neutrality is theoretically impossible. Viewed in this way, we understand that any reflected judgment about any social phenomena, including mediation with two disputing parties, always arises out of elements of relatedness and less-than-conscious conditions. As such, we can never understand other human beings except in terms of our own, and their relational context. Instead of pursuing questions about "truth" and the "right," we can shift our inquiry to the contents of consciousness of the mediation participants. We can also look for ways to discern to bring the unconscious to awareness. In short, we can disentangle some of this embeddedness; for that which we cannot disentangle, we can work within it.

This notion of relatedness includes ideas that subjectivity itself arises out of relational context, that whatever we think we perceive is always a process of relation; there is never just a foundational perceiving subjectivity that perceives an independent object.[12] They are together as part of a process. Second, there is the notion that an individual consciousness—a perceiver—is always a part of a larger framework of related consciousnesses, i.e., other individuals. There is, therefore, no such thing as atomic individualism [Descartes's proto-foundationalist view]. Third, and perhaps the most scintillating and useful concept, is that all individuals in a relational field, i.e., mediation, are co-responsible for its effects. This leads to the discourse of inter-relationalism, which I will build on in future segments of this model. This is part of the existential psychoanalytic model that I have been constructing which, I believe, has useful applications in cooperative conflict resolution practice such as mediation and collaborative divorce law processes. It also figures prominently on one variation of classical psychoanalytic theory. I will develop these ideas further in the text that follows.

II:
History of the Modern Self As A Way to Understand the Mediation Process

This chapter discusses basic ideas about mediation only in the most condensed of ways because there are many mediation books on the market that explore in painstaking detail these methods and processes. (For example, see Colatrella's Mediation: Skills and Techniques or The Practitioner's Guide to Mediation by Stephen Erickson). As a part of this summary, I aim to explicate further the historical and cultural conception of the self, starting with Descartes finishing with Freud, Lacan, and related theorists. Let's address a few basic concepts in mediation at this point.

Mediation is the process by which at least two conflict partners and a "neutral" person mutually contemplate conflict issues and their resolution. Theorists usually present a series of helpful principles; theories about conflict; alternative methods; and a methodology that is described in terms of stages. These stages usually include setting structure, building trust, fact-finding and clarification, negotiation, do-able steps and implementation, and final agreements. Often, these theories address personality, cognition, emotion, behavior, needs, and communication, which support the expression of the methodology that is chosen.

In a previous work (Essays on Phenomenology and the Self, Essay Three), I present a criticism of the type of self that has emerged from the modern period in the western culture. This is critical to our discussion; it is central and mandatory that we deconstruct the type of selfhood and subjectivity that we have created in our culture because it is at the very base of my argument—even though this is not strictly polemic—that we cannot solely rely on our conscious intuitions for professional practice. Instead, we must interrogate, intra-personally, the very orientation with which we approach professional transactions. As I have argued, this requires a deeper phenomenological analysis of the possibilities of self, self-consciousness, and interpersonal interactions.

In early modernism, we jettisoned ourselves from God, feudal oath, and traditional interpretations of life, putting ourselves into conditions of uncertainty, and later accommodating our anxiety with new allegiances to calculative certainties as a way of life. In a sense, it was a rapprochement of the Athenian questions posed centuries before, including the possibility of knowledge, our place in the universe, and valuations about human interaction. As our belief in the church faded our belief in empiricism grew strongly. This also extended to psychological, moral, [and later] professional issues and questions, in which the quest for justification became a matter of nature and human science.

In the Medieval period, the "self" was largely anonymous and undifferentiated in consciousness outside its place in the matrix of church hierarchy and located-ness within it. All focus was on meeting external proscriptions, i.e., following the rules, which left little for the construction of interiority—the experience of self-consciousness and responsibility for calculating morality. As ecclesiastical authority waned and the Reformation occurred, the focus on the objective world for behavioral answers gave way to the construction of a new subjectivity—self-inwardness.

Descartes, Locke, Hume, Montaigne, Rousseau, and Kant, therefore, were working within these unmoored conditions of great learning and scientific advancement, theorizing about the extent and conditions of knowledge and its justification. They discussed questions of truth and reality, the existence of good and evil, and the nature and place of humans in the universe. They explored the relation between mind and body, whether accurate representations of the world were possible, and how a science of psychology could be constructed. Perhaps more importantly, they called traditional values into question and discussed truth and morality without appealing to God and the Church. By separating the answers to these questions from questions of value, we humans left ourselves without a transcendent foundation. This lack created the conditions for continuous ontological anxiety except as it is covered over by self-deceptive strategies that involve hiding the truth from ourselves— even though those truths have a tendency to affect others.

During the Renaissance and the early modern period, the Church became fragmented and divided over the Reformation. Mercantile capitalism became more prominent and individualism emerged. These changes influenced the breakup of the religious-military-economic structures at the foundation of feudalism. With increased interest in the study of humans the privilege and authority of the Church was threatened. These new interests also threatened the power of the new nation states that countered with new forms of punishment and control (such efforts producing structural ideologies of truth and knowledge). Thus, the need arose to develop an intellectual justification for the new science of empiricism and to explain why its techniques should be used in moral deliberations instead of those at the Church. Society became less certain about questions concerning morality and value. This further increased anxiety amongst human beings.

People of the early modern period needed new moral guidance and intellectual justification for the overthrow of the relations of power of the Middle Ages. Early modern philosophers came armed with the science of empiricism and ideas about innate rationality, thereby enjoying the success of the physical sciences. In the sixteenth, seventeenth, and the eighteenth centuries, humans had a strong belief that science would solve their confusions about the natural and social worlds, especially about the universal laws of human nature, morality, and value. Locke and Hume, for example, believe that empiricism could discover the truth of human beings whereas Descartes, Leibniz, and Kant argued that it human rationality that would provide such foundations. Other thinkers such as Rousseau and Montaigne argued that we ought to use the mirror of nature as our guiding force instead of the techniques of science. All of them agreed, however, that we could achieve our sought after explanations and understandings because of the capacities of the human mind, the efficacy of reason and nature, and the superiority of observation and logic over tradition and dogmatism. We left ourselves, therefore, on a quest for new foundations in our interpersonal and intrapersonal experience.

Both Hume and Kant decided that an empirical science of psychology was impossible. Hume argued that we should not accept explanatory concepts such as causality or the unified self because they cannot be demonstrated empirically. Kant responded by arguing that although humans cannot empirically demonstrate certain concepts, they can perceive them. Therefore, the capacity to perceive these concepts must be implanted in the mind. Kant thus invented modern structuralism, an important paradigm in 20th Century social science. He argued that we naturally possess perceptual structures that allow us to categorize and organize the phenomenal world. In contrast, the noumenal world is beyond our grasp. Because humans can only see through these structures, scientific clarity into the workings of the human mind is not possible.[13] (See Kant's Critique of Pure Reason)

Even so, philosophers, scientists, and other thinkers began to use the new sciences of modernity in human affairs and moral guidance. This strategy involved the relations of power between the Church and modern science. By replacing the old structure of the Church with a new one, leaders reconstructed a new worldview through the use of new terms and relationships. For example, concepts such as freedom, scientific truth, objectification, and personal responsibility emerged as manifestations of the new human individualism. This new framework of power relations (which I will explore in a later chapter in this text) carried along with it a program of self-surveillance, self-transformation, self-objectification, disengagement, inwardness, and radical reflexivity—and an ideology that we were capable of such matters. With the valorization of this new worldview, a struggle began over the phenomenological structure of human beings. It was the modern self that is at the cynosure of these power struggles.[14] Because the focus of the creation of value changed from an external source to an internal source, a great deal of pressure was placed on each individual to account for one's construction of value. This began the agonizing human struggle to discover the source and method for the determination of value.

In short, the change in the configuration of the self from the Middle Ages to the Modern era included the removal of God, the development of objectivity, the universalization of doubt, development of interiority, and the prioritization of rationality. Thus, instead of locating value in Platonic Forms or God's law, Descartes and others relocated the source of value and meaning in individual rational agents. By utilizing the proper logical procedure, humans could construct an order of truth with certainty and therefore build a foundation for knowledge: this was his proposition concerning methodical doubt. This was allow us to live in accordance — morally and ontological—within that truth. In this belief system, the most important capacity, which orders the universe and to direct human behavior, is located inside each human individual, and therefore shifted responsibility to each of us.[15]

Descartes removed God from the material world, keeping him in the realm of the spirit. Although the realms of the spirit and materiality interacted with each other, they were separate. The material realm takes up space and the spiritual world does not. According to Descartes, because the material world was disenchanted it must be dealt with on a different basis. He therefore advocated a "scientific" attitude with an objective stance toward it. This required humans to emotionally remove themselves from the world of matter in order to study it mechanistically and understand its functions. This discipline of inwardness and emotionless logic implied that no traditional body of knowledge, including that of the Church, had any prior claim over a scientist or philosopher. This led to further anxiety over foundations because these underlying forces must have exerted a great deal of pressure on the self to constitute a world, thereby, assuming itself as the source of meaning and value, constructed through rational strategies.[16]

Universal doubt[17] and logic were of the highest priority. Human bodies were of the material world; as such, in order to gain understanding free from emotion, we were required to objectify it. This would enable us, therefore, to dominate our bodies with our minds—through self-surveillance. For Descartes, for example, we could discover the logical order of the universe by carefully inspecting our innate mental functions, which are also the source of morality. Inwardness thereby took over as the locus of moral authority. Ironically just as natural-world scientists proved that the center of the universe was not the earth, Descartes and others argued that the center of the moral universe was in each individual—shifting Archimedean points in opposite directions. This furthered conditions of anxiety even more because we had nothing to rely on except our "reason," which could come to many different conclusions and was, therefore, insecure like Church doctrine had become. More dangerously, by prematurely accepting one's rational conclusions, one could cover over the uncertainty in value caused by our transcendent ontological nature. It is my belief that this strongly led to the development of what I call the "possessive self," in a previous work.[18]

Locke took some of Descartes's ideas, such as objectification, and thematized them in a way that eventually led to modernist notions of psychology that were based on quantification and categorization. He applied these ideas not only to the material world but to the mind as well, treating it reductively as another manifestation of the natural world. He proposed a methodology of radical disengagement that resulted in the instrumentalization of the natural world, the self, and others. One must disengage from the self in order to remake oneself. In so doing, one becomes an Other to oneself, which creates a new relational dynamic that is based on teleology and use instead of deontological regard.[19]

Instead of proceeding in accordance with the Church, this new set of power relations valorized the remaking of the self in accordance with scientific discipline, especially Newton's ideas about bodies and motion. At this time, both scientists and philosophers determined that instrumental control via mathematics and physics was the road to truth. Along these lines they tested hypotheses for their ability to predict and control human behavior. Thus there was a link between these new formulations of the self and the need for governments to have control over their populations. Locke was a radical empiricist and applied this system to everything, including the human mind. He argued for a kind of radical reflexivity whose goal was to reconstruct the self in a way that was based on sensory experience. This was possible for him because even ideas were of the material world and this was a realm humans could control.[20]

With regard to morality, Locke believed that we must act independently from tradition. Locke's idea of self-responsibility comes from this assumption that we can stand back from ourselves with a critical and objective eye in order to remake ourselves. This disengagement became one of the hallmarks of modern science because it allowed us to assume control over representations of the world. Perhaps the most important point here is the extreme egocentrism that arose. By locating power and agency within each individual, wherein the self is the final arbiter of truth and the center of moral motivation (and personal comportment), Western individualism arose and developed as a formidable adversary of the Church. It was a hidden question whether this reflexivity was as radical as the culture thought it was.[21]

In contrast to radical empiricists such as Locke, others thinkers such as Rousseau and Montaigne founded their arguments in the transparency of the external, natural world. In contrast to the promotion of disengagement and objectivity, they committed to delving even deeper into the interiority of subjectivity. Even though thinkers in this camp did not espouse rational disengagement, they did support the new individualism instead of Church authority. Montaigne valorized the uniqueness of each individual, disagreeing with the scientific method of objectification, seeing chaos where others saw order. He added this truth of inner chaos and instability to his arguments against the dogma of the Church, asserting that the chaos of the deep interiority of the self disproved the possibility of one universal set of laws of human nature. For Montaigne each person is unique, chaotic, and multi-faceted rather than stable and universal.[22] He believed that external standards of morality were not applicable to humans because these traditional standards did not take individual differences into account.[23] They treated everyone the same as if we had a universal human nature. Given this assumption, we gain self-knowledge by learning about our uniqueness through introspection. Instead of objective disengagement from the external world we should adopt an even deeper subjective engagement in order to find the truth of our natures. The naturalists, therefore, provided us with a different sense of the concepts of freedom and autonomy, and wove them around the valorization of individuality instead of universality.

Rousseau took up Montaigne's program of introspection and the understanding of one's limits and perfected it as a complete antagonism to the Church. For him, we can find out who we are by listening to our inner voices. This will guide us as we try to understand how we ought to live. Whereas Augustine had looked inside and found absence, which he eventually filled with God, Rousseau looked inward and found the sole source of unity and goodness to reside deep inside a fully autonomous, individual self. Unfortunately, this idea of autonomy was not based on a firm foundation but one that was alienated from the lived and natural experience of humans. Kant later argued that the laws of morality were limited by the very nature of reason, which was imbedded in the innate structure of the human mind. For Kant, morality did not spring automatically from the objective methodology of the new empirical science or naturally unfold from the subjective, inward encounter with the transparent truth of natural being. In contrast, morality comes from the rational will and is one of the innate structures of each human being.[24] He agreed with the naturalists that we must follow what is generated within our subjectivities. He agreed with the rationalists that it is only out of universal doubting and the exercise of human reason that humans can figure out how to live. With Hume, he argued that sense experience alone is unable to generate foundational concepts and moral laws. Once can see here the attempt to re-fashion God as foundation by substituting in a rational apparatus that is provided by the universe.

Kant argued that moral knowledge is more than pure, natural impulse generated from within. He also argued that it is more than what we can perceive from outside us, in terms of pleasure and pain. Instead, moral knowledge is produced from the innate structures of rationality and agency. He believed that humans were the only animals that can use the logic of these innate structures to generate moral laws and then to choose them through acts of will. Like Hume and Montaigne, he believed that freedom just is living in accord with what one truly is. Yet he also held that individuals are not limited by an unstable or empirical nature. Instead, he believed that individuals are liberated by their nature because they have been given the structures and will that could actually lead to the true moral laws.

Kant thought he had saved the epoch from its own contradictions by maintaining freedom from traditional authority, reaffirming autonomy, and upholding personal uniqueness. Like Augustine, he believed that a transformation of the will saves an empty individual. However, in contrast with Augustine, instead of God being the force that fills the internal void and transforms the will, it is the universal structure of rationality that facilitates this transformation. As I mentioned, it is highly questionable whether this move gets us beyond Church doctrine in the formation of value. Kant's developments took one more step toward the valorization of an isolated, interior, individualist self. This modernist self was powerful and autonomous, but it was removed and isolated from the outer world. Presumably, this meant that it was also isolated from other humans, caught up in its own rational machinery. It was capable of building the order of the universe from internal logic and sense impressions. It had achieved independence from the Church through radical doubt, observation, and objectification. Here, spirit was divided from body, which became a disenchanted world. Further, this self could engage from this divided world and achieve scientific self-certainty and self-sufficiency. It was a self that was made of instrumental, independent consciousness, and it could therefore transform itself. It took this deep strategic relation and applied it to the natural world and perhaps most unfortunately, also to the social world. It was one thing to apply the method of objectification to the natural world, but when it was applied inter-subjectively to other individuals in the realms of value and morality, we see the beginning of egocentric social structures.[25]

As we mentioned, it was also the Romantic era of the eighteenth and nineteenth centuries that asserted a belief in an autonomous individual who had the capability to determine its own destiny. Individual uniqueness and the notion of the mysterious, hidden self became a source of vitality and self-potential. This notion of interior mysticism became a source of secular salvation but when combined with the rationalist notion of objectification also contributed to egocentric social relations in which the instrumentalization of others was foundational.

III:
Two Directions the Self Took in Relation to Modernity

In order to develop our account of the three basic models we can use to analyze mediation dynamics, we need to explore—in short—the historical developments that led to these new conceptions. The first delineates some of the major developments of that self from the medieval period to the present (which involves the new philosophy of mind that includes an unconscious element).[26] The second includes phenomenology, which arose around the end of the 19th century in Europe, and which offers a new ontology about the foundational relationship between self and world. By summarizing these new theoretical shifts in the theory of the self, we will have more clarity about developing models of analysis for mediation and negotiation encounters.

First, there was the development of a new philosophy of mind that included an unconscious element.[27] In the Medieval period, the self or subject behaved in accord with various rules that commanded behavior in a feudal and theocentric world. As such, humans were objectified and occupied structural positions within the fabric of society. Moral action was not complicated but one only had to follow certain proscriptions. However, toward the end of the 15th century, all dimensions of the ecclesiastical system started to wane, which gave rise to the emergence of a proto-subjectivity that was based on a sense of a personal "I," free [to some extent] from the Church. This new awareness of a personal self motivated scholars, thinkers, and scientists to create and discover its new riches, both as fact and as value. Moral focus migrated to the power of the autonomous self to make independent decisions, and one's salvation depended on it.

However, as individualism developed and the questioning of authority grew to gigantic proportions, the focus shifted from a criticism of human science issues to the criteria within which we could examine the issues in the first place. In sum, we became concerned with the conditions of knowledge and truth, doubting our senses, perceptions, and thinking apparatus.[28] Near the end of the 17th century, though, Western history took a decisive turn with Descartes's rigorous proto-foundationalist account of knowledge that was based on the existential subject who could doubt. In the Cartesian framework we cling to our own illusions of autonomy, and this is the self that has dominated the western ontological landscape, although now de-stabilized by other claims to truth about the nature of the self. Descartes founded modern science, both human and natural, through his methodology of doubt; however, at the same time, thinkers like Moliere showed the split between one's being [one's unconscious aspects] and one's speaking subject [demonstrating perhaps an early formulation, or at least acknowledgement of the inauthentic self].[29] Even so, the dominating view of the self regarded Descartes's Cogito as the "true" or authoritative view about the modern self.

Romanticism added another perspective about the self. It originated in the Renaissance and was Cartesian because it enframed the self as an "I," a centered and unified self that could constitute a world. In contra-distinction to the ratio-centric self that Descartes envisioned, the Romantic self—unified and centered—navigated emotions, intuition, creativity, and imagination in a way that purported to transcend the scientific weltanschauung of the day. Unfortunately, Romanticism was often tied to individuals whose perceived madness or social deficiencies, and therefore did not become the center of what was considered normal, as a measure of social rationality and practical reason. Moreover, the influence of Newtonianism and proto-structuralism [naturalist accounts of human being-ness that begged determinism], which won scientific and political favor, only served to further strengthen pure Cartesianism and all derivative rationalisms.

We see, then, how the construction of subjectivity—the self—moved from the certainty present in the Medieval period to a deep and unstable abyss over the next several centuries. There was too much data regarding the lack of control most of us had over our lives to ignore; too much irrationalism that did not cohere with the predominant, Cartesian rational ideal that needed to be explained. Let's focus right in on the philosophy of mind that Descartes spawned: it was a mind—a masterful, lucid, and transparent one that could predict and control a natural and social world.[30] Thus, at the time Freud emerged, we had several conceptions of the self that all included the common idea that it was unified, self-aware, rational, and could exercise its will on the world through choice. At this time, many scientists, scholars, philosophers, and other thinkers were overly impressed with this Newtonian-Cartesian self-construct grounded in empirical science, strongly believing in the transparency and objectivity in one's own perceptions. They also, and perhaps just as importantly, believed in the possibility that perception can accurately envision the world, that consciousness really can perceived the truth of reality. This began the rule that empirical science has had over all other scientific approaches, continuing to this day and beyond.

It is my belief that modern, contemporary professional life overly valorizes this conception of the self—the transparent, masterful, rational Cogito, at the expense of a broader and deeper phenomenological experience that either concerns a shift in ontology (which I will address in the next section) or a philosophy of mind that includes an unconscious element (See my book Essays on Phenomenology and the Self, Essay 1, for such an argument). My goal in this book is to render a preparatory analysis of this new approach, first by exploring the historical transformations in subjectivity that make this possible, then by analyzing new models for professional practice that take into account a broader and deeper phenomenology of the self. This will, in my opinion, create more ethically sensitive practice and more astute practitioners. Although I have outlined the Freudian meta-psychology in another work (Essays on Phenomenology, Essay 1), I want to point out some of the main axioms and tenets, which will then enable us to compare the Cartesian self. In addition, let's be clear that there have been several developments of empirical psychoanalysis since Freud, such as Object Relations, Inter-Relationalism, Cyclical Dynamics, and Lacanian Theory, but I will include these developments in my presentation of the practical analytic models and not in this historical section. I think it is also advisable to wait to address these developments until after I account for the type of mediation to which my models apply: as a prelude, I can say that I want to focus on transformative mediation processes, and not so much on rights-based, evaluative, or even mere needs-based mediation. Although these types and approaches to mediation are important and valuable, I am more interested in presenting an account of the possibility of fluid relational change in the mediation itself, which in my experience simultaneously addresses needs, rights, and evaluation.[31]

Within Freud's metapsychology—his architecture of the self—there is his philosophy of mind that includes both conscious and unconscious elements. He bases his theoretical edifice around sexuality, arguing that it is central among internal stimuli. For him, humans are primarily

motivated by libido—drives that push us to action, both consciously
and unconsciously. The mind, under this scenario, is an apparatus for
discharging stimuli that impinge upon it, including external and internal.
The structure of the mind, along these lines, is to contain that stimuli and
eventually discharge it. The most central of the instincts are the sexual,
including libidinous tensions that come from all parts of the body, and
which create relational associations, such as the craving in the infant
to suck on the breast of its mother. Body objects, therefore, become
sexual motivators—libidinal objects. Each libidinous object at various
times in an infant's development becomes the organizational locus of
these relational connections [or in some parlance, object connections],
taxonomically distributed as oral, anal, phallic, and genital.

Freud's metaphor was archaeological, which allowed him to search
for unconscious, fully formed intentionalities that motivated attitude,
emotion, and behavior.[32] Since sexuality was as the bottom of the
hermeneutic enterprise, the search became one for childhood sexual
experience—erotic attachment to the primary caregivers, one's
interpretation of it, and what was repressed into the unconscious.
Childhood sexual impulses show up in adult life disguised as neurotic
symptoms and undisguised as perversions. As a matter of mental health,
these impulses are sublimated into alternative forms of gratifying
behavior, for example, anal impulses into disorder or tidiness depending
upon one's childhood experience.[33]

The algorithm, as it were, of Freud's theory was the Oedipus Complex,
which is an explanatory model that helps us understand complex intra-
psychic dynamics relative to one's father and mother. In this metaphor,
children form desires and attachments to the opposite-sex parent and to the
same-sex parent as a crucial developmental step toward adolescence and
adulthood. According to Freud, the complex is resolved through castration
anxiety, which becomes, derivatively, the ego ideal and superego, holding
primary impulses in check throughout life. According to this line, each
person's version of the complex is unique, depending on a number of
genetic, hermeneutic, and environmental factors at play. It becomes a
structural blueprint for one's interpersonal possibilities for a lifetime.

I want to highlight Freud's philosophy of mind because it is a radically different worldview than the Cogito, which we get from Descartes. In it, what we experience—our conscious awareness—is but a small part of the mind. The unconscious, which is the other part, is not translucent and is therefore hidden. Unfortunately, this means that we largely unaware of most that motivates us to behavior, feeling, and cognition. Thus, in opposition to the position that we constitute meaning consciously, this position holds that most of the meaning that one person—one self—constitutes, is largely out of awareness. That is, our normal, everyday sense of awareness is an illusion, opaque, and a plaything of unconscious forces according to the Freudian worldview. Our belief that our minds are rational processors of external data is actually a product of the confluence of impulse and defense. How we normally deal with life as adults is always a codified struggle manifested by compromise formations that are underwritten by unresolved [political-sexual] struggles within the Oedipal complex.[34]

As Freud developed his theory of repression, he made it clear that these self-constraints were not just to keep sexual desires at bay, but more to keep destructive, harmful impulses from hurting others—so that society could survive and hopefully flourish. Repression, viewed in this way, is not a negative process, but more of a set of regulatory decisions that operated for the benefit of oneself and others; the tricky part of formulating and understanding this theory is to gauge the dialectical balance between too much and too little repressive societal controls. At bottom, the conscious self is a compromise—a consequence of intra-psychic and interpersonal conflict.[35] We learn in the history of psychoanalysis that these conflicts can and do create split-off and unconscious parts of ourselves that motivate us to action without our awareness. Now that we have taken a brief, introductory look at Freud's changes to prevailing views about structure of the mind/self, we can move to a similar exegesis about the phenomenological view about the self.

Second, we see the developments from Brentano, Husserl, Heidegger, Sartre, Merleau-Ponty, and others. We will see, and I will try to account for, a continuation of the Cartesian Cogito, but a shift in understanding of the relation between subject and object—metaphysical dualism. Phenomenologists had to bridge the gulf between the empiricist and intellectualist traditions of the past centuries. They believed that neither empiricism nor intellectualism sufficiently faced the human situation. By concentrating on one pole of the I-world relation that is given in consciousness, they distort this relation and fail to explain human existence in terms of the fact that we are always with others. Man interrogates the universe but is also an inherent part of that universe. There are two views that attempt to understand the nature of this relation. Naturalism treats man as a being that is determined by physical and material factors that determine him from the outside. In contrast, idealist intellectualism views man as having a liberty in constructing representations of those same causes that act upon him. The problem arises because man is part of the data that he tries to understand.[36]

Contemporary naturalism tries to understand the higher, the spirit, in terms of the lower, which is the subhuman universe. While the phenomenologists do not directly attack positive science they do argue against the assertion that the only truth is scientific truth, which is by definition unverifiable. They attempt to reduce the field of truth to one mode of understanding, and it is this move that the phenomenologists attack. In contrast, intellectualism attempts to interpret the lower in terms of the higher, because it believes that the higher gives the lower its sense. It is the attempt to reveal the rational structure of the world by considering its intelligibility independently of any reference to sense experience, as a sufficient source of knowledge.

Naturalism is a critical empiricism that is either psychologism or positivism. In the former, all human truth derives from sense impressions. For the latter, all truth comes from positive scientific truth. Phenomenologists argue that both forms are abstractions that are laid upon pre-scientific contact with the world. This is lived experience. Sense impressions and scientific "facts" are thereby constructed upon the lived world of natural perceptual experience. These objects represent only a portion of the totality of our lived experience, leaving out our primordial experience of the aesthetic, social, and moral domains. For a phenomenologist these objects are not the primary datum. On the other hand, intellectualism mistakenly holds that philosophical reflection is the primary guarantor of truth. Yet there is no idea that does not refer to some perceptual experience from which it has been abstracted. Reflection is always a reference to a pre-reflective experience that preceded it.

Existential phenomenology tries to show that both of these systems are mental constructions and that the better method is to return "to the things themselves" (Husserl's famous axiom).

Another problem of naturalism and intellectualism is that by reducing truth to a single mode they make man's relation to the world unintelligible. Naturalism cannot account for one's temporal experience of oneself within a world of meaning-creating activity. In a naturalist model, meaning comes from a world of pre-determined causal forces and not from an individual who looks to the past or to the future in the domain of possibility. Thus, this approach completely neglects the meaning-giving activity of each of us as a free consciousness that can change his or her interpretations of experience. Intellectualism is also a false anthropology because it reduces a person to a bodiless spirit, a disembodied thinking substance. If man is just embodied spirit then he is an alienated interiority without access to the world. Without a link to the world we cannot account for how this interiority manifests itself as exterior, nor could we account for intersubjectivity. Let's now turn to a more developed discussion of mediation itself, to prepare us better for an examination of how these new theories about the self must be examined and utilized by the mediation practitioner.

IV:
An Idea of Mediation that Goes Beyond Needs and Rights

It is my thesis that mediation in its present form — at least all that I am aware of — rests on the modernist notion of the self: masterful, self-transparent, rational, and such, the Cogito.[37] More importantly, this is the double view that the self is a thing that can be studied like other things, in terms of mechanistic process; further, it is the view that we can have objective views of things in the world, such as other selves.[38] For mediation, this results in the view that a person has rights; it also results in the view that a person has needs and preferences that can be determined and utilized in interest-based, collaborative and cooperative mediation processes.

Mediation typically follows a step-by-step logic that includes the following: creating an effective atmosphere, clarifying perceptions, focusing on individual and shared needs, building shared positive power, learning from the past while moving forward, and generating viable and mutual options. It involves shifting the worldviews of the conflicting parties from an adversarial, competitive dynamic toward an orientation that prioritizes cooperation, mutual benefit agreements, and positive and constructive behaviors. It involves the overcoming of ineffective approaches including conquest, avoidance, bargaining, the quick fix, and role-playing, and replacing these alienations with a conflict partnership approach that favors mutually beneficial outcomes.[39]

An essential element to this approach is to break conflict down into its component parts. By doing this in some way, the conflict partners can adopt a reflective approach that overcomes emotionally-reactive tendencies, and dialogue about these component parts in a positive and constructive way that benefits both and which honors the their relationship, whether or not it is ending or continuing. This involves respect for difference, attending to the needs of both, clarifying perceptions, moderating and balancing power, being sensitive to important values and principles, honoring strong feelings, and probing into internal conflicts. The ontological structure thereby shifts from a dualistic, "I versus You" approach to a "We" orientation that supplies both the relationship and the individual parties with their needs and preferences. A skilled mediator can facilitate these shifts in orientation in ways that the parties might not ever be able to accomplish themselves.[40]

Mediation processes, whether in divorce and family, small business, or larger organizations, start with information gathering and an initial meeting, ending in some kind of Memorandum of Agreement. Between the beginning and the end, there are several variations in methodology, and different cases have different requirements; therefore, there is no "one size fits all" approach, in my opinion, as long as the mediator and parties are meeting the mediation objectives. Initial consultation establishes the tone and mood, and educates the parties to the process, along with important considerations that will help drive toward the goals specified. In the modernist framework that I specify above, this process is typically framed in practical terms, but in my approach I argue that it involves deep, unconscious networks that can be explained and understood in terms of psychoanalysis and phenomenology. This is the import of this book.

The initial meeting (or meetings), either joint or mutual, involve the sharing of facts, answering important questions about relational behavior and dynamics (whether professional or personal), the sharing of the mediator's background and approach, the rules about disclosure and confidentiality, and the expectations and steps involved in the process. This also includes a fee statement, any questionnaires (if agreed upon), and any other housekeeping documents the set the terms between the mediator and the clients.[41] Mediation can occur in one day or a couple of days; it can occur over several days or weeks; it can also occur over a longer period of time if the matter is complex and involves multiple parties. I personally have experienced mediation processes that either occurred over the duration of a year or a period as short as ninety minutes. Again, there are unconscious elements to all of these aspects, the way they are presented, and the way upon which they agreed.

The sessions themselves can vary in length, frequency and number. Traditionally, mediators set rules about comportment and protocol, and some with the participation of the parties. Obviously these rules are designed to maximize cooperation and mutual regard, but human communication and behavior is complex, and it is my thesis that there is much in our experience that happens unconsciously, in the phenomenological field. Thus, even if we pay mind to constructive rules of engagement, we lose precious information if we disregard the unconscious elements, as I will continue to explain. In addition, the practice of taking notes and presenting the parties with summaries of sub-agreements from previous meetings, while a good one, must be tempered by sensitivity to the mediator's own unconscious biases, anxieties, and practical limits lest they sediment the process, rendering it paralytic and distortive, as I caution. The culmination of the process is a set of verbal agreements that become memorialized in a Final Memorandum — hopefully minimizing unconscious elements that can move the process in distorted directions, away from the autonomy of the participants without their being aware of it because of stress and anxiety.[42]

Questions about the role of the mediator and the assumption of neutrality involve a complex set of issues and answers that, in my opinion, emerge from the historical account I presented earlier, which involves a certain way of viewing the self, especially in relation to dyadic encounters (and for our purposes this includes professional encounters). In short, mediators facilitate the goals of cooperative conflict resolution that I outlined earlier, including the construction of a conflict partner alliance. Because they are not personally involved in the specific conflict, it is believed that they can contain all the irrationality, emotion, and aggression of the parties and facilitate cooperation for mutual gain. In sum, a mediator can move conflicting parties from their instinctual, limbic brainstem processes to the higher ordered cerebral cortex — this promotes reflection, and not reaction. This doesn't mean that the mediator solves the problems of the conflicting parties; he or she just maximizes the positive relational and psychological conditions that can lead to such resolution. This also does not mean that the mediator understands the conflict partners' dynamic as an objective phenomenon.

It is said that mediators must connect empathetically with each client, manage the emotional and practical issues, and properly address each of the issues by utilizing mediation tools he or she has learned from previous experience and training. Each of these elements assumes a Cartesian cogito, i.e., that adults are more or less self-aware, autonomous, and can make rational decisions in their best interest while cooperating with their conflict partner; this includes the mediator. Within this worldview, the mediator is self aware enough to contain volatile emotions in the conflict parties, as well as any personal biases that may arise, which happens. Of curse, there are techniques that can help create and develop emotional connection and rapport with clients, but this stance assumes that the mediator is perfectly self-aware or aware enough to know the impact that her own emotional sharing will have. It is also true that to some extent, this works. However, if we assume a different philosophy of mind that includes unconscious content, then we must question the level of autonomy, intentionality, and control that a mediator has when he is fostering these sorts of emotional connections. We must find a way to confirm that the process remains untainted from any undisclosed or unresolved issues that a mediator may have that could infect the process. We must also be wary of the premise that each client is similarly fully aware or sufficiently aware to appropriately understand his or her emotions and their impact on the mediation.[43]

Aside from building these emotional connections that engender a level of trust necessary for adequate facilitation, mediators generally help do the following: identify and clarify issues; help the analysis of options and their consequences; develop discussions about fairness of the issues, choices, and outcomes; manage the cooperative process through to a written draft and necessary reviews. All of these aspects are accomplished in terms of the history and context of the parties and their conflicts with careful and usually open questions that are designed to clarify the issues and possibilities for their resolution. Strategic and tactical questions can help reveal unacknowledged conflicts that the mediator might see when the parties don't.[44]

What is more problematic is whether a mediator can be neutral; if she cannot in principle, then we must determine how a mediator can deal with that lack in a way that supports fair, comprehensive, and effective resolution. It is generally agreed that if a mediator is not neutral then he cannot be fair. It has also been thought that a neutral mediator can facilitate a fair process by balancing power imbalances and other distortive factors. This traditionally occurs through the application of basic techniques and tools in the process, as well as by an awareness of a mediator's own biases and value judgments. In short, we have generally believed in the assumption that a mediator can be neutral because of the way we have viewed the self and the way that we have viewed science. I believe this is at the root of the (mis) belief that we can "balance" power dynamics.[45]

In the main, within a modernist scientific paradigm, we have had the assumption that an observer could be neutral and could make a so-called objective judgment about the data before her. This view has percolated into the rest of our lives, including professional practices in the law and in psychology, which include the belief in clear and accurate objective judgments. This underlying set of assumptions has also held true in mediation. Trainings and educational programs have and do work within this framework—within this conclusion—that mediators can be neutral and have "objective" judgments, and offer comments accordingly. Thus, there are mediation ideologies about being "clear about one's strong feelings and values," "working through biases," and "not allowing oneself to be swayed by comments that trigger one's own issues." This is all fine and good, and such technique is headed in a corrective direction. However, these techniques and trainings all operate within a certain set of assumptions about the self, science, and relational dynamics that are no longer persuasive.

I am not focused on the problem of whether a mediator can overcome biases, prejudices, and other phenomena about which a mediator is fully aware and with which one can easily be trained to deal; I am speaking about deeper aspects of the self that can only be revealed with a) a philosophy of mind that includes an unconscious and various psychoanalytic models that utilize these philosophies of mind to reveal unconscious phenomena in ways that are practically useful and ethically recommendable and b) a philosophy of mind that, while assuming a conscious mind, includes theoretical architecture that reveals how we engage in self-deceptive strategies that effectively hide important mental content.

The current view is that the idea of mediator neutrality is a regulative ideal that can be practically approached asymptotically through education, training, introspection, and dialogue with colleagues, in order to fully engage in corrective action. Deviations from absolute neutrality are viewed as opportunities for education and further training. This, as I have mentioned, stems from a certain kind of worldview that we have inherited from western modernity—from the Cartesian weltanschauung. It is my belief and argument that this worldview is insufficient because it leads to false beliefs about neutrality that would not ever be considered unless we postulate alternative worldviews. This is the cynosure of this prolegomena. However, I do not wish to engage purely in negative dialectics; as such, I propose these new models as roadmaps to re-interpreting [false] neutrality. I believe that our very biases and prejudices can be useful if properly examined.[46]

Current mediation techniques, education, and protocol are well justified and effective, but only within the underlying meta-psychological parameters. I believe that if we question these parameters, through the use of the sciences of phenomenology and psychoanalysis (which I will explore later in this text), which allow us to see other meta-psychological possibilities and structures, we will be able to entertain a fuller range of phenomena. This is a scientific criticism and comes from scientifically based research and clinical practice, both in psychoanalysis and in mediation and other cooperative conflict resolution domains such as collaborative law and facilitative conflict management programs. The fundamental groundwork, therefore, involves critically exposing the limits of the Cartesian self and replacing it with a conception of the self that allows us to see a wider and deeper range of self and relational phenomena. This includes the idea that the self is not static; it is dynamic. It is not singular; it is multiple. Derivatively, we can entertain a mediation logic that moves beyond needs and rights that are based on a static conception of the self, toward a mediation process that is more transformative—both inter-relationally and intra-relationally.

V:
Transformative
Mediation

Transformative mediation involves a different conception of the self, so let's take a look at that first. Instead of a unified, fully translucent self, we ought to consider a plural or multiple self that at times might be difficult to discern. Under this view, the self is not a thing; instead it is a complex system of processes, both conscious and unconscious.[47] This implies that needs and preferences are not static and that they can evolve during an actual mediation process. This allows us to make a criticism of the view that needs and preferences of an interest-based mediation can ever be reified into a closed set at any one point in time. In contrast, because the self is not viewed as a thing; because it is a plurality of forces and voices; because each participant in a mediation can never be totalized as an objective phenomenon; and because a person can and often does have evolving perspectives about his needs, mediation can be viewed as a transformative process. Let's explore this view; it will be important in our investigation of the different psychoanalytic approaches that rest on it.

Let's first review some of the characteristics of a cooperative mediation process in summary form. This will help us to understand the idea of transformative mediation approaches that utilize philosophies of mind that include unconscious elements. Some mediation is evaluative, often conducted by a mediator who has substantive matter expertise in the matter at hand. I am not speaking of that type of mediation because it has a different set of expectations that emerge from prioritizing the mediator's substantive interpretation of legal issues that affect the rights of the parties.[48] In contrast, I am focused on the sort of mediation that is client-centered and while being sensitive to legal rights and substantive issues, focuses more directly on interests, needs, and preferences that may both converge and diverge from the law.

In typical client-centered mediation, the mediator facilitates what both parties consider to be a fair outcome, focusing on their joint and several interests. It is future oriented, requires mutual benefit agreements, and allows for flexible options and corrective solutions as additional conflict issues arise. Instead of viewing power as a force that allocates rights and responsibilities, it is viewed as a relational good to be shared. Instead of focusing on the law it focuses on the parties in the room and the development of their ongoing relationship. For example, parents can work out a cooperative parenting agreement that doesn't put the parties at odds by one party being the custodial parent and the other party the visiting parent.[49]

The process is not viewed as a competitive contest with winners and losers. Instead, every conflict issue is viewed as an opportunity for relationship building or at the very least, for trust building that can inure throughout the rest of the mediation process. Battles are turned into mutual benefit agreements regarding specific issues, which create shared positive power. It is also often the case that battling parties do not immediately realize that they have significant shared interests. These transformative processes involve replacing old, dysfunctional thinking, speech, and behavior by new ways that promote the mutual interests of both conflict partners. As a part of these goals the mediator promotes non-threatening and honest communication; provides reality checks that overcome anxiety; discourages blame by refocusing on future goals; encourages neutral and positive language; motivates the parties to brainstorm for new solutions; creates trust and a climate for resolution; and encourages fairness, assertiveness, and positive thinking.

If we then focus on the mediation process itself we notice a) that there are big differences between litigation and mediation; b) that there are substantial opportunities to transform the process from an adversarial one to a cooperative one; c) that within a cooperative mediation process itself, there are significant opportunities for transforming the self systems of the conflict partners, their ostensible needs and interests following, as well as the relational dynamic between them. In this sort of radical process, the end result of a successful mediation can be very different from what the parties argued for in the beginning. I believe that by utilizing both conscious and unconscious content from mediation and relevant dyadic interaction, a mediator can help the conflict partners to refine their process with even greater accuracy and efficiency. In short, by looking at less-than-conscious elements in himself—largely unconscious propensities—and by noting those of the parties, a facilitative mediator will have a deeper and more accurate interpretation of the conflict

situation; by using this more complex hermeneutic approach, a mediator will have more tools with which to facilitate a successful process.
The converse of this is also true in my experience: by not looking at unconscious or partially conscious elements, a mediator can diminish her ability to facilitate the best possible mediation outcome.

Let's focus on the transformative process itself that mediation can provide. It can create conditions for cooperation, positive and constructive dynamics, and mutual and reciprocal outcomes. The question at hand, then, is how this can occur. Most people, I have discovered, have difficult, negative, and dysfunctional attitudes toward conflict. Often, people associate it with anger, fear, failed relationship, destruction, control, power, and related feelings. Cognitively, individuals often perceive it as a disruption of order, a win-lose battle, definitive of a whole relationship, or a struggle between the true and the false or the bad and the good.[50]

Transformative mediation processes attempt to change these belief systems into those that are more positive, constructive, mutual, and cooperative. Part of this is to move adversarial dynamics into cooperative dynamics, but there is much complexity in theory, practice, and technique required in order to make this happen. I believe that the psychoanalytic models that I will present in later chapters of this book can make a valuable contribution to that theory, practice, and technique. In the main, transformative processes convert dysfunctional, anxiety-rid, power-seeking dynamics into positive and constructive communicative and behavioral patterns that valorize mutuality and reciprocity. Again, I believe that the deeper the mediator's insight into her own unconscious propensities, the more efficient she could be at facilitating more functional dynamics between conflict partners. Without taking these complex elements into account we mediators lose precious and valuable data—both process and substantively oriented—that can substantially enhance the quality of the resolution process. Let us continue this exploration.

There is a complex unconscious penumbra to all conscious experience that operates as a constellation of connections between emotion, cognition, and behavior. When conflict partners begin a mediation process, they bring with them a relational system that needs help; that is why they seek voluntary mediation. Part of what they bring is an expectation that a mediator can help them sort through these difficult dynamics and create an environment that leads to satisfying resolution. Central to this new environment is a process—led by the mediator— that transforms the process into these aspirations and regulative ideals. We can divide this transformative process container into at least three dimensions as follows: First, there is the goal to maximize each party's ability to make fully autonomous decisions; second, there is the goal to create conditions for mutual empathy and genuine reciprocity, with both emotional and cognitive elements; and third, there is the goal to produce fully transparent and radically honest communication in a way that recognizes difficult and challenging less-than-conscious elements. I say less-than-conscious in order to accommodate both classical and existential versions of psychoanalysis, which we will discuss in the next several chapters. I believe that by maximizing individual and joint autonomy, empathy, and reciprocity/mutuality, a skilled mediator can guide and facilitate the conflict partners to the best possible outcome.

I think that it is helpful to consider the evolution from modernist conceptions of the self to postmodern conceptions. In modernism, autonomy of thinking was the highest value, as we suggested earlier. Implied in this value, however, is an individualistic framework that in this domain prioritizes rights. In later conceptions of the self, primarily constructed in the 20th and 21st centuries, there is the new value of relationship and relational paradigms. A review of the psychoanalytic, psychological, and philosophical literature clearly shows the emergence of a priority in a belief and valorization in the relational self and relationships in general.[51] Thus, protecting rights of individuals, while important, must be integrated with the newer conception of the self and its concomitant value of relationship.[52]

For example, most conflict mediation work is between parties who have ongoing relationships that they desire to continue, whether in families, businesses, or other organizations. For those conflict partners who will not be continuing a relationship, we increasingly find the desire to terminate in good ways with good feelings, including trust and respect.[53] It is no longer as simple as protecting rights or focusing on "interests"; it is now more about relationships and how they figure in one's future life that is becoming increasingly important. In moral theory, this is exemplified by a consideration of new values such as empathy, care, concern, and solidarity, alongside older virtues such as rights, needs, autonomy, agency, and the like. This requires the mediator to have done his or her own psychological and emotional work (or to be doing it currently), and to be sensitive to unconscious relational forces, coming from all directions in a mediation process. It is also important to consider the profound power that there is in dialogue between two conflict partners who are contained in a mediation process. I have found that much mutual benefit can emerge in dialogue that neither party nor the mediator could have ever imagined possible. We will address this further, later.

Let's set the stage for discussion of the psychoanalytic models I will present and discuss. As such, it is important to consider the complex psychological dynamics that come with the inception of conflict that brings two people to court or to a mediator. I have discussed some of the negative or disempowering beliefs that many people have about conflict. In short, most beliefs are negative and disempowering; as such, this is how people begin conflict resolution processes. This can include lack of trust, uncertainty, distrust, confusion, doubt, anger, hostility, inability to see interpret accurately the behavior of the other. Through the sort of resentment that can occur in failing relationships, the parties can become unable to see who their partners are except through eyes of anger and pain; this makes it nearly impossible to work through conflict issues in an honest and transparent way.

Conflict transformation requires a change in dynamic, and what is exciting is that newer models of subjectivity actually view the self as much more plastic and changeable than older models from the Enlightenment. If these newer models are persuasive or at least plausible, we can start to see how taking unconscious data into account is possible — and helpful. Look at the elements of destructive, negative communication, in terms of word choice, tempo, whether utterances are in the indicative or interrogative, whether the trajectory moves to the past or to the future, how each partner is regarded, and so forth. Compare positive dynamics, which are significantly different in quality. These different dynamics manifest themselves and their phenomena can be studied. An experienced mediator can move these dynamics from a negative quality to one that is more positive. This requires some self-knowledge, good technique, and a willingness of the mediator to engage in the process. An experienced mediator constantly looks for entry points so as to facilitate these shifts; as such, less-than-conscious or even conscious content can provide valuable clues as to these entry points, as well as to the type of solution that a mediator can exercise.

Now that we have delineated a broad summary of mediation, the idea of transformation, and the different conceptions of the self, we can take a look at some of the sorts of interventions and participations a mediator can engage to move the resolution process into a positive and constructive dynamic. This sets the stage for probing further into the psychoanalytic models I propose.

Mediator participation and intervention requires attention and focus, and a communicative toolkit that allows the "neutral" to facilitate directional changes in the conflict resolution discussion, the goal being to transform negative dynamics into positive ones. This requires, as I mentioned, a parallel transformation from the assumption of a radically individualistic self with rights and needs to a relationally oriented self who has emotional and connective requirements, too. This requires great skill in a mediator who can help presence the natural elements in human beings for empathy, mutuality, and reciprocity. This requires shifts in ontology from self-other adversarial orientations to you-me/we orientations that always take both parties into account equally. Greater psychoanalytic awareness in a mediator can promote these shifts.

Communicatively, there are a number of standard moves that a mediator can and might make, both to proactively drive a cooperative dynamic and to facilitate course corrections along the way if necessary; a passive mediator is just as dangerous as an aggressive one, and we recommend assertiveness in a way that augments the autonomy of the participants. Here is a partial list of contributions a mediator can make. I mention them because I believe that each and every one of them can be enhanced through psychoanalytic exploration by the mediator—of herself and of the participants.

Educating the participants about the rules, considerations, and suggestions for a successful resolution process is essential; likewise, educating about the sorts of behaviors and communications that would likely lead to failure is equally important. By outlining expected outcomes of various approaches, I have found that most adults can problem solve individually and jointly in sophisticated ways; it is the educational phase (and preparatory psychological phase) in mediation and other forms of cooperative resolution that greatly helps overcome the reactive tendencies of the instinctual, lower brain stem. Having dynamic options and brainstorming, solutions-oriented process from the outset can move most parties into cooperative formats. It is also important to take preliminary expectations of the process and explore them, providing alternative ways of thinking about various issues. This means that an experienced mediator will not take a passive position; instead, he takes an active participatory role to widen mutual possibilities, both for discussion and for resolution. This, of course, includes communicative strategies that facilitate the reflection and introspection. Just moving the parties into reflective positions has profound effects on the process.

In his verbal participations, a mediator is sensitive to tone, feeling, and emotional heat, organizes and summarizes, points out differences in interpretation, leaves space for additional reflection, allows for anxiety and confusion, stays out of the discussion as much as possible, highlights areas of agreement, asks questions that are designed to clarify, supports efforts toward empathy and mutuality, helps the parties to understand the destructive impact of trigger words or destructive patterns in communicative exchange. It is also important to become aware of non-verbal communication, and proficient at intending bob-verbal communications that facilitate positive and constructive resolution.54 Again, it is my strong belief that if a mediator utilizes a philosophy of mind allowing for unconscious phenomena, he will be much more astute in his participations and interventions in communicative exchange, and that much more effective in his meditative goals. Let us now proceed directly to discussion about the psychoanalytic models.

VI:
Model A:
The Existential
Psychoanalytic Approach

In this approach, there is no (reified) unconscious per se, but there is the belief that we engage in strategies of self-deception whose effects appear and function as an unconscious.

When we explore the Existential Psychoanalytic approach—which involves a pre-theoretical phenomenology—we have to consider the underlying beliefs we have about the self—what a person is. As I mentioned earlier, we have been primarily influenced by Descartes' powerful analysis of the self as a thinking being that engages an objective world that can be studied and understood. By using a phenomenological approach we can see that this rigid subject-object structure is only a way of seeing but not a hard fact about the world. We can also question, therefore, the assumption that an impersonal observer (a professional mediator) could, with the right kind of method, discover the truth about the nature of reality (by being "neutral" in a mediation process). However, the phenomenological approach, when applied to human existence, holds that no subject knower can fairly exclude herself from the phenomena that she studies. According to this view, there is no radical split between subject and object and therefore no way to ever obtain objective, detached truth about the nature of the universe. I believe that the same logic applies in a professional setting such as mediation: one's professional judgment is always colored by the phenomenal field, unconscious data, and even the mere interactional components between all elements, including the parties, the mediator, the setting, and the circumstances.

If we consider the phenomenological worldview, we assume that any knower (or professional mediator) is always embedded in a complex of interrelationships in the social world. In fact, even walking into a mediation session [or any social encounter] affects the mediator in ways that may go beyond his or her conscious awareness. It also affects the other individuals in the room in ways about which they may not be fully aware. This is the point of each of the psychoanalytic, existential, and linguistic-structural approaches. They interrogate this penumbra at the margins of awareness and understanding in ways that can bring important content and data into consciousness for the mediator. Without taking into an account the possibility of structural elements that escape conscious awareness, we can miss important information that could be used to deepen our understanding in a professional encounter.

In the very late 20th century and early 21st century, the scientific movement in phenomenology began, which started to change—albeit slowly—our worldviews about the nature of a person's relationship to others and to the world at a very basic level. It was through the work of Brentano, Husserl, and Heidegger that we started to challenge the Cartesian view that we could see the world in an objective way and make rational judgments about its nature. Instead, we started seeing that the subject-object distinction is just a possibility of being; it purports to be basic when in fact it rests on a more primary orientation of being-in-the-world, which is how we explain our embeddedness. In short, phenomenology suggests that any interpretation of mediation as being neutral or as having objective insights as a result of his experience is an illusion. Part of the received argument is that if a mediator is neutral and other safeguards and processes are put into place, then a mediation process is fair. I am suggesting that in principle [at the ontological level] a mediator cannot be neutral, but that this does not negate the possibility of a fair process. Viewed in this way, we can understand that any reflected judgment about anything, including two disputing parties, always arises out of elements of relatedness and connection. This includes the relationship between the conflict parties, their relation to the mediator, and each person's intrapersonal relationship with himself or herself [i.e., the psychoanalytic]. Within this view, we can never understand other human beings except in terms of our own, and their, relational context.

This notion of relatedness includes the idea that subjectivity itself arises out of a relational context, that whatever we think we perceive is always a product of relation; there is never just a foundational perceiving subjectivity that perceives an independent object. They are together as part of a process. Second, there is the notion that an individual consciousness—a perceiver—is always part of a larger framework of related consciousness, i.e., other individuals. There is, therefore, no such thing as atomic individualism, even in a professional context. Third, and perhaps most scintillating, is that all individuals in a relational field, i.e., mediation, are co-responsible for its effects. This leads to the discourse of interrelationism, which I will explore further as we traverse my continuing ideas. This leads us directly to the existential psychoanalytic model, Model A, which has direct application to professional mediation practice. I will now further explore this model, which I will follow in successive chapters by discussion of classical psychoanalytic and linguistic-structuralist models.

Because the approach I am offering is new to mediation and other cooperative conflict resolution processes, I will proceed by outlining various questions and issues, and the beginning of a theoretical model with clinical and practical applications. First, we are never isolated human beings; we are always in the world in relation to others, our selves, ideas, feelings, nature, and so on. Second, what we take to be our individual subjectivity does not exist in a privileged, Cartesian space. Instead, it emerges only from a relational matrix. Third, all individuals within a relational context are co-responsible for the phenomena that occurs within that context. Let us proceed further, keeping firmly in mind that we are addressing the assumption in most mediation handbooks that a mediator must be [and can be] "neutral." I will now engage in informal and preparatory discussion about some of the assumptions that I believe, in actuality, refute the notion that a mediator can ever be neutral, unbiased, and unprejudiced—or would want to be.

It is axiomatic to the existentialist view that we always live in conditions of uncertainty. That is, we always live within two self-components, which are the ontic and the ontological. The ontic is roughly the way our ego engages character-logically, forming self-identities professionally and personally. The ontological is the open, transcendent, self space that each of us has to make different value and behavioral choices as we go forward. Furthermore, we never have a complete view of any situation; we only have a perspective. As such, we are always being-in-the-world in conditions of uncertainty.

As such, how we interpret that uncertainty becomes very important in triadic and more complex conflict resolution encounters. As Heidegger shows us in his early work (Being and Time), we are always in a mood.[55]

We always care about the world in various attitudinal orientations. For example, I could enter a mediation tired, sad, joyful, hopeful, or in many more simple and complex moods. As existential phenomenologists generally believe, these moods and orientations determine the way in which we interpret present experience. Furthermore, because we are always in conditions of uncertainty, we always move forward within anxiety, a situation from which each of us makes individual choices — complex or simple depending upon one's history, the current environment and relational context, and a number of other factors. Finally, the way we construct meaning in a mediation or other conflict resolution process is never simple; it always involves a multi-factorial ontological account of the way a particular mediator is interpreting experience, what she hears, what she says, relative to her own emotional and cognitive situation in the present.

It is also the case that each person in a conflict resolution encounter has a different and unique worldview that, I believe, ought to be carefully analyzed in preparation for any mediation or collaborative process, before actually engaging. Let us discuss some of the considerations of the assumption that each person has a different worldview and how those considerations could affect a mediation process. There are three elements to a worldview analysis, including constructions of the self, the Other, and the world.[56] These include elements of the self such as beliefs, values, feelings, meanings, assumptions, and the like. They contain attitudes, beliefs, and behavioral propensities toward others. They also contain attitudes, beliefs, and values about the physical, social, cultural, moral, and spiritual aspects of the world. Other existentialists such as myself frame these orientations as social, personal, natural, and spiritual, which are inter-connected dimensions through which we each create a world and a worldview. What is most important for cooperative conflict resolution practices, however, is to understand that there is a complex worldview that each person brings into the mediation encounter. I'd also like to point out that while mediation has been traditionally a one-session or few-session process, that is changing and being replaced with much longer and more extensive methods. I have participated in transformative mediation and other collaborative resolution processes that have taken up to one year.

Bridging the complex differences between worldviews, therefore, requires the "neutral" third person to engage in an existential-ontological analysis of these different worldviews in an efficient and educational manner that provides momentum for the process. This careful reflection requires trenchant semiological analysis of the way each person, including the mediator or neutral third uses language.[57] Even without difficult major, cross-cultural considerations, the skill of integrating all the beliefs and values that are somewhat hidden in language and word choice requires great powers of discernment and attention.[58] Again, this takes time, and a competent mediator must find a way to engage in this dialectic—the back and forth hermeneutic process—that will actually facilitate fair and speedy resolution. It is my belief that the phenomenological method is the best possible way to approach unknown individuals in their quest to solve their differences. Let me then use some space to outline the most basic elements of the phenomenological method as the primary toolkit for creating a reflective semiological equilibrium in these resolution processes. There is a vast and complex literature associated with the science of phenomenology, but it all starts with a few basic methodological assumptions. It is these assumptions that can help us engage in an existential psychoanalytic approach. In the main, however, let us know that phenomenology arose as a reaction against the theory-ladenness of Cartesian-Newtonian-based positivist science, which assumes a transcendent and fully aware investigator [professional]. While it is important for a mediator to understand the facts, it is equally important for her to understand how the parties interpret and understand these facts.

The three assumptions are as follows: First, we must bracket all of our assumptions, biases, and prejudices—our expectations—in order to focus on the primary data of our experience. This would mean to approach the mediation encounter with something like "beginner's mind," in a way that allows a fuller and more accurate receptivity of the conflict in the room. One can quickly see how an analysis of the inter-relatedness of worldviews and existential dimensions can be critical. Second, the "neutral" third person must refrain from engaging in [internal] explanation in terms of various theoretical considerations he or she might favor. For example, the mediator would hesitate to engage in a quick personality analysis as a way to engineer facilitation. Instead, the facilitator-mediator would, internally, commit to extensive description of the social phenomena in front of him. This is not to say that this would be shared communicatively, but it would be part of the existential presencing that the mediator would bring to the table. Third, the neutral third party would refrain from placing any data into some sort of hierarchical analytical structure. This is sometimes known as the "equalization rule," which gives all comments and all phenomena equal weight as a strategy to avoid prejudice, bias, or tendentiousness in the facilitation. This helps avoid any "sedimentations" or self-deceptions — unresolved issues — in the person of the mediator, which could throw the process out of a fair equilibrium. We will approach later how a mediator's unresolved issues — to the extent of their lack of resolution — can easily create a distorted mediation or cooperative conflict resolution process.[59]

VII:
Model B:
The Classical Psychoanalytic Approach and Its Three Variations

Now that we have initially addressed the existential psychoanalytic approach, which I call "Model A," we now turn to a classical analytic approach. This view, which I call "Model B," includes three variations; they are different versions of the same model because they have a common philosophy of mind that includes an unconscious. Before I delve into Model B, I want to stress the importance of an analytic approach to mediation and other cooperative conflict resolution processes. After painstaking research and thousands of hours of clinical practice, I feel confident to say that there is much experience that can escape conscious (or "attentive") awareness. This can greatly affect our confidence in the proposition that there can actually be a neutral third party in any of these resolution processes; at best, the notion of neutrality ought to be deconstructed and re-developed into a more refined concept that includes awareness of those processes at the periphery of consciousness. It is my belief that without a fuller awareness of them, so-called neutrals can often affect the outcome of resolution processes without choosing to do so, and sometimes in often-hidden and negative ways.

There are three basic approaches to Model B, the Classical Psychoanalytic tradition. They are 1) Freud's drive theory; 2) the relational approach (positivist); and 3) the cyclical-contextual paradigm. Let us now turn to Freud, keeping firmly in mind that the classical approach includes a theory of mind that believes in a dynamic unconscious that motivates speech and behavior.

In a Freudian psychoanalysis, consciousness is reduced to an epiphenomenon of unconscious forces guided by scientific laws of cause and effect. It looks for unconscious forces behind conscious experience for explanations that lie outside that experience. In this paradigm, our basic motivation is the pursuit of pleasure and the avoidance of pain, which returns an organism from excitation to equilibrium, which is known as the principle of constancy.[60]

In his economic hypothesis, Freud uses the metaphors of charge and discharge from modern physics to explain psychical forces in terms of neurophysiology, explaining the connection between the psyche and its objects and the formation of neurotic symptoms. Freud assumes that libidinal energy is the main motivational force of each human and uses this idea to explain normal development and pathology in terms of conscious and unconscious energetic displacements and permutations. For him, the meaning of normal and pathological development is located in the neurons and not in personal choice and the self-creation of meaning. The connection between consciousness and objects is a mechanical paradigm that can be measured, thereby reducing psychopathology to neurophysiology. Most importantly, for our purposes, his theory of equivalence explains that whatever is repressed in consciousness is activated in the unconscious.

In contrast, to Freud, relational theories eschew drive discharge as primary and instead favor the notion that ties to others—important early relationships—explain later psychological phenomena in a more accurate and comprehensive way. They often have criticized the idea that there are fully formed mental contents sitting in our unconscious that motivates us to action. One of a handful of these approaches stresses the importance of interactional representations that are linked to early ties to parents and other caregivers. According to this approach, in early childhood we develop beliefs, values, expectations and affects in accordance with these early interactions and our interpretations of them. They become hardwired or structuralized as internal object relations before there is even a differentiation between self and other and, as such, exist at a profoundly foundational level in the psyche as one ages. This structure carries with it social expectations and strong affective themes such as love and rejection, self-esteem, abandonment, vulnerability, intimacy, and autonomy. In this alternative archaeological view, psychopathology is a product of negative self-representations that produce distorted and unproductive representations of oneself, others, and the social word, thereby leading to unfulfilling relationships in adult life. This leads us to the third view, which has been discussed by Paul Wachtel in a caring and considered way.

The third variation of the Classical Psychoanalytic approach is the cyclical-contextual model, which is also a psychodynamic approach that assumes motivation can spring from an active unconscious. Wachtel (in Relational Theory) argues that this is not an archaeological approach of stripping away defenses and resistances in order to arrive at an inner core that was wounded thereby creating distorted cognition and affect. He is keen to point out that both drive theory and object-relations theory focus on primary relationships in childhood and the relation between patient and analyst. However, he thinks it is important to include issues relating to other [present] relationships, and additional factors such as race, class, culture, ethnicity, and gender.

Even though this approach assumes a personality structure, it believes that this structure is not explanatorily causal but instead can be affected by current relationships; he is clear to point out a fluidity between self and other that allows for bi-linear causalities and effects. A fortiori, even though there is self-structure in this approach, it is the context that determines which organizing principles of the self will come to the fore and actually organize social experience. With even more intrigue, this approach believes that we draw into our pathology the individuals from our current life; they become accomplices in holding together our assumptions and expectations [note that Sartre, even though an existential psychoanalyst and philosopher, discusses brilliantly this drive for accomplices in his section entitled "Concrete Relations" in his Being and Nothingness.][61]

Thus, even though we are set in motion at an early age with a certain self-structure, that self-structure itself can be affected by other people in various contexts, as we go forward. In short, we engage in presencing ourselves as different people in different contexts.[62] This is why it is so important to gain information, perspectives, and interpretations of the parties' current relational "matrix," for this can illuminate a number of details about how each of them relate to their conflict as well as their unique possibilities for resolution. I will discuss both "accomplice recruiting" and "concrete relations" (which involves some ontological discussion of sado-masochistic relational dynamics in a later chapter, and its impact on mediation).

Let us see how important this Classical Psychoanalytic approach is to mediation and other cooperative resolution processes from the standpoint of a "neutral," third person. First, if the mediator is unaware of the effects of any of her unresolved psychological issues — her pathology, as it were — distorted phenomena can easily occur in the process, whether viewed from a perspective of drive theory, relational theory, or cyclical dynamics theory. Second, specifically focusing on the third variation, if it is true that different contexts trigger different aspects of each self — each person — in a mediation process, it is critical that the third-person "neutral" become as aware as possible of these effects, his own pathological distortions [the unresolved issues!], and the psychodynamic issues of the parties involved. If we disregard this level of analysis, we risk untoward, unexpected, and unintended distorted consequences. I will explore further these distorted effects in later discussions of Michel Foucault's trenchant analyses of power and Jean-Paul Sartre's theory of sado-masochistic socio-psychological dynamics that can occur in ostensibly "neutral" professional settings such as mediation, negotiation, and collaborative law.

VIII:
Model C:
The Structural-Linguistic Approach, Part 1
(Foucault)

We have now looked started to question the possibility of a "neutral" environment in mediation from a psychoanalytic point of view. Let us proceed further into this approach by examining some of Michel Foucault's ideas about the structural relationship between power and knowledge. This will give us additional insight about the less-than-conscious distortions always latent in a phenomenal field extant in a mediation transaction. Let me clarify at the outset that Foucault is not a psychoanalyst. However, his ideas on language, structure, power, and knowledge can help us understand the psychoanalytic vision of Jacques Lacan, who we will address in the next chapter. It is also true that Foucault's perspective about structuralism sheds light on psychoanalysis in general because psychoanalysis is a kind of structuralism.[63]

Foucault's deconstructive type of approach challenges voluntarist philosophies such as Sartre's [existential approach] by showing us that what may appear to be rational autonomy and free choice might not be so at all. This should cause us pause in our approach to any resolution process that appears to be neutral. That is, the apparent semiological structure of cooperation according to Foucault's approach might hide pre-structured relations of power that give one side the advantage over another, depending upon all the diverse factors I have pointed out before, including culture, race, ethnicity, gender, socio-economic status, and the identity of the neutral, third person who is present.[64] Let us now take a look at some of these ideas with the objective of challenging the proposition that there can ever be neutrality in cooperative conflict resolution processes, including mediation.

In his later work, Foucault concerns himself with the processes within which humans are made into subjects. He replaces Sartre's notion of a transcendent, constituting subject (the Modernist subject) with a version of the self that is constituted by relations of power.[65] In Foucault's conception, there is s docile aspect of the self that is created by the effects of power. There is also a resistant aspect that can resist power by avoiding the will to truth and, instead, create new forms of subjectivity.

In Discipline and Punish, Foucault offers a genealogy of the modern individual as a docile and mute body by presenting the interplay of disciplinary technology and social sciences with their standards of normativity. Here, he argues that individuals are socially constructed, based on categories produced by the relations of power in the human sciences. In Discipline, he gives an account of the modern history of power from the seventeenth century to the present, showing how power has evolved from being primarily repressive to the current condition where it is mostly productive. By the nineteenth century, power emanates from all levels of society, producing various effects along with the repressing of behavior, a structure that he calls "biopower."

The two main strategies used in the new disciplinary technology are surveillance and normalizing judgment, which places each individual into an objective category and evaluates him by how far he deviates from the norm in any particular way. These strategies force individuals into certain roles in society and account for each person's place in the disciplinary grid. Deviations from the norm are punished so as to correct for improper behavior. Most individuals accept these roles and live by them, although others engage in strategies of resistance. For example, Foucault argues that in the nineteenth century (applicable to 20th and 21st) the bourgeoisie became concerned with the promotion of healthy and productive bodies in their eugenics projects, in order to prevent the degeneration of their class. The working class was forced to maximize productivity, which meant that forms of sexual behavior always had to be evaluated by their relation to capitalism and the underlying interests of the aristocracy. Behavior that promoted production was considered normal; behavior that was pleasurable for its own sake and which did not add to economic productivity was branded abnormal and subject to correction.

The phenomenologists and the structuralists influenced Foucault's ideas even though he was neither one himself. It is his beliefs about power that ties these influences together and synthesize competing claims about explanation in the social sciences, thus I need to say a bit about what he means. For most of the 20th century, the debate in the social sciences has been between those who see power as exercised by individuals and those who see power as a result of structural factors within systems.

Voluntarist theorists view power as being exercised by individuals. Structuralist theories view power as the result of the structures within systems. Foucault attempts to synthesize these contrasting positions by showing that there are two levels or perspectives of power, and that both agency and structural factors have an explanatory role. He presents us with the intriguing view that "power relations are both intentional and nonsubjective." His objective is to study the effects of power, and he does this by focusing on how power is exercised rather than how it is possessed and by whom. In contrast to Marxist theories of power, which hold that power is a substance that can be geld, Foucault adopts the Nietzschean position and is nominalistic about it. Power, for Foucault, is not a thing and cannot be possessed. Instead, it is the name we attribute to a complex strategic relation in a particular society. I believe that mediators can be trained to analyze to a helpful extent the strategic relations between disputing parties and the strategic relations that inform their very subjectivities. This is part of the very thesis I propound in this book.

At any point in time a society is structured by a set of rituals of power that create asymmetrical relationships between humans. Foucault analyzes this web of unequal relationships by focusing on how people relate to each other on the most local and interpersonal of levels. Relations of power are thus immanent in all kinds of relationships. Further, power does not come from the top and trickle downward; instead, it emanates from all directions and, I have said, is productive. Because he believes that power relations are intentional and non-subjective means that they can be explained from two perspectives. He believes that these relations are always imbued with calculation, aims, and objectives. Yet, this does not mean that power is necessarily exercised through the choice of an individual subject. A well-informed mediator can facilitate greater autonomy in each disputing party. This leads to greater sustainability of the mediation resolution.

At the local and tactical level of political activity there is conscious decision-making; intentionality is present. Here, individuals are aware of what they do and every act is planned and deliberated. In contrast, at the structural level, which is the underlying matrix of power relations, there is no subject. Exercises of power are not the result of anyone's direct, conscious planning. Thus, relations are non-subjective. This means that even though agents are aware of their decisions, the broader consequences of local actions are not planned or coordinated. There are results that are beyond the intentions of any one agent. Yet, these patterns, which emerge historically, have logic. They are the result of the underlying strategic interplay of all the unequal relations of domination. The direction of these local practices is provided by the underlying technologies of power that instantiate a particular society at a particular time. Foucault's intent is to analyze these tactical practices.

He argues, then, that there is a government of power relations that limits individual actions in various relationships. It is a structure of previous actions that conditions possibilities for future actions, providing a context within which new actions can occur; it guides a field of conduct and in a sense orders a range of potential outcomes. Thus, at a mostly unconscious level there is a structure that governs a field of tactical behavioral choices. Rational agents, therefore, have a range of choices delimited and made possible by the underlying power structure: to some extent this applies to cognitions, emotions, and perhaps imaginations. This structure changes through history, sometimes as a result of successful resistance or by the transgression of previously established limits.

Foucault links power relationships and their inherent potential for reversal by arguing that they are unstable states and can easily rupture into each other. These relationships of power are reciprocal relationships of struggle. They limit each other and each is always the possibility for the other. It is the region of struggle that can be explained by the purposeful actions of a subject. When struggle reaches its limit, though, and becomes a relationship of power, actions are better explained by structure, not by subjects. In a power relationship, the nature of that particular relationship determines the limits of behavioral choices each individual has. These individuals are not, according to Foucault, traditional subjects who are their own ground of choice. Instead, the structure of the relationship determines the choices. Thus, even though the behavior of the individuals involved is intentional within the power relationship, this intentionality is grounded within the matrix of power operating within society at that time, and further refined by the specific relation of power involved. It is interesting to note that even good mediation does not dissipate power.

It can show it and thereby help the parties become more aware of the dynamics that they are in and the dynamics they need to move toward for fair and sustainable resolution. Yet, nowhere can we get rid of power, and I am not sure that so-called "balancing of power" improves the situation. It is the awareness that leads to constructive and positive cooperative agreements.

According to Foucault's way of thinking, one's personal identity, therefore, has a relation to truth that carries with it substantial political implications. Foucault shows us that what passes for ultimate truth is dependent upon our historical circumstance and the power relations underlying them. Thus, we have regimes of truth that vary with historical time and place. Furthermore, it is the production of truth that constitutes who we are. For example, we can try to locate ourselves within the categories of psychopathology, relying on various measurement tools and practices such as the DSM. Foucault argues that we are subjected to these games of truth by the power that individuates human beings. Being subject to means that one is subjected to someone else's control and that we are tied to our identities by conscience or self-knowledge. Both meanings suggest a form of power that subjugates humans to scientific knowledge. Individuals are forced into a connection with knowledge and power makes certain that we are dependent on that knowledge for our identity. My subjectivity arises, therefore, from the recognition of myself. Because we each have both docile aspects that are manipulated and resistant aspects that can influence change, we have split and divided selves that presence socially, always subject to standards of normativity.[66]

If we accept Foucault's belief that power is embedded in the very way we speak — usually without reflective perspective — we must be suspicious about what appears to operate both normatively and epistemologically. This includes conflict resolution processes such as mediation. On the issue of neutrality, psychoanalysis points out that what appears one way may actually be codified intention about something else, that there are unconscious forces that can be difficult to discern or decipher. This applies to any setting of one's life, including the professional mediation context. Given this account, mediators ought to consider the sort of language that is used in the parallel action, the language the parties use to describe each other, and the language that the mediator uses with them.

These languages are part of a dimension of the underlying relationships of power that structure the dynamics in the mediation itself.

IX:
Model C:
The Structural-Linguistic
Approach, Part 2 (Lacan)

Now that we have taken a look at Model C, from a Foucauldian perspective, let's turn to Lacanian psychoanalysis which, in some senses is like Model B—the Freudian approach—but more so it is a structural linguistic approach so I include it her as part of Model C.

In order to understand Lacan, we must realize that he follows Freud by accepting that there is an unconscious element in the self. However, Lacan bases his theory of the unconscious on language and transforms Freud's pronouncements about the family and the body into assertions about culture. For him, psychoanalytic theory becomes a study of the construction of the subject in language. Repressed unconscious desire becomes the search for meaning in language. The symbolic father of the Oedipal struggle becomes a set of power relations imbedded within language. (See Ragland-Sullivan's book, Jacques Lacan and the Philosophy of Psychoanalysis and Bruce Fink's book, The Lacanian Subject)

Lacan believes that the unconscious can only be accessed through speech and writing. He is interested in Freud's dream analysis and techniques of free association, and he argues that the unconscious is structured like a language. In his quest, Lacan appropriates Saussure's linguistic theories in order to conceptualize the unconscious as part of an endless chain of unconscious meanings that we can find only in language in the spaces between conscious meanings. He modifies Saussure's structural model of meaning by arguing that there is an endless signifying chain from the conscious construction of meaning down to the unconscious, which constantly reveals itself in language.

For Lacan, it is the interdependence of both the words and the gaps, such as hesitations, blunders, and sighs that endow the whole system with meaning. No signifier can signify can independently of other signifiers; it is the differences between them that give the meaning. For example, "love" has a different meaning from "live." Standing at the limit of the differentiations of meaning is material plenitude or totality, including psychosis and death. This is the realm of the "Real." Recall that Freud uses to concepts to interpret dreams, including displacement and condensation. Lacan transforms these Freudian terms into his own linguistic paradigm, labeling them as metaphor, which is the identification of one known with another known, and as metonymy, where a part stands in for a whole. He argues that these two concepts explain the connections between signifying chains of conscious meaning.

According to Lacan, subjectivity emerges from these strings of interconnecting meanings and structures in language. Personal identity arises from the way personal narratives are created within these meanings. This Lacanian subject is always inhabited by the Other, which is comprised of all others and other significations within the overall linguistic structure. The subject always carries around the Other with it and has no inherent substance, personality or traits of its own. It is, therefore, dependent upon the intersubjectivity embedded in language for its very existence. In contrast to the object-relations theorists, the subject is not an empty container that gets filled up with objects, including its relations with others. In fact, signifying processes are seen as a series of events, and the construction of personal identity takes place through these events. Further, our view of the world is always constrained by the pre-determined meanings that exist. It is a linguistic algorithm of sorts through which we interpret the world.

The complete linguistic structure in which one lives is the universe from which one's self can emerge; the danger is that we can never step outside these pre-determined meanings, which act as Kantian filters and mediate our experience of others.[67] They are our very foundation in being. Thus, we can only interpret reality in terms of the language that we use, the language that speaks us. Further, it is through our use of language in our search for knowledge that we live our repressed desires. Intersubjectivity is made possible by the emergence of repressed desire in language, which propels us from one meaning to another. In fact, we achieve repression through language by driving our unconscious desires downward into the space between words, in our speech acts. Thus, language at both the conscious and unconscious levels operates as the possibility of freedom, personal identity, and the attainment of truth because it offers an infinite range of interpretations of our experience.

Lacan rejects the object-relations idea that our identity can ever be authentic or coherent. He asserts that our identifications only lead to a sense of identity, not an actual identity, but that it is always based on misrecognition. In addition to the Real, Lacan divides his structural theory into two parts, including the Imaginary and the Symbolic. It is within the Imaginary and the Symbolic realms that we create ourselves. Using Freud's idea of primary narcissism, Lacan asserts that when we are infants we initially exist in an undifferentiated ego mass with the mother. Eventually, within this morass of emotion, sensations, and drives, we begin to sense that we have a distinct self with definable boundaries. This is the realm of the Imaginary. Yet, this identity is always based on an image of oneself that is reflected back from someone else, much like the reflection from a mirror, which he calls the "mirror stage." The person we usually identify with at first is our mother, but although this sense of identity appears real to us it is not because it depends on something external. This early sense of identity comes when we feel, unconsciously, a coherent sense of self through the eyes of the other, even though otherwise our self is dissipated and dispersed. In this state, our self or ego is never our own because it depends solely on our identifications, including people, things, and ideas.[68]

Lacan also argues that we establish another kind of identity, what he calls subjectivity. We acquire this new kind of identity in the Symbolic realm as we acquire language. Here, we think that the apparently fixed meanings in language give us a much more stable sense of identity, and we look for the truth of who we are in language. By believing that these relatively stable meanings can give us some coherence to our identity, we attach ourselves to the way we define ourselves linguistically. Yet, even in the realm of the Symbolic we do not gain the stable sense of identity that we want. The unconscious reappears in the spaces between words. There is always a gap between our unfulfilled wishes and the language we use to convey identity and desire. This means that for Lacan phonetic relationships between words are more salient than semantic ones. They may reveal unconscious meanings that are different from the conscious ones.

Our belief that there are stabilized meanings always runs the risk of being de-stabilized by unconscious desire and early loss. There is always a gap between the conscious "I" that we construct and a deeper, unconscious sense of who we are. Lacan seizes upon this assumption and argues that our conscious identity, which we formulate through the use of the regular and conventional categories of language, is always false. The identity we create through language, in the Symbolic realm of consciousness and culture, is only another reflected identity without substance. For him, it is no different than the imaginary one we created in the mirror stage, in the Imaginary realm. Thus there is the pre-verbal bodily identity that we construct in the mirror stage in the Imaginary realm; there is also the one that gets constructed in the social, cultural Symbolic realm. Lacan's argument is that we psychologically invest in false images of ourselves in both the Imaginary and Symbolic realms. He believes that there is a fictional element in the construction of our identities from the ground up, and he utilizes Freud's theory of narcissism and stress on language as a form of the mastery of early loss. Yet a major distinction between the two concerns how they view the status of the ego. For Freud, the ego really is a substantial self that can develop from a primitive state of narcissism. In contrast, for Lacan the ego is always false because it is based on reflections in the Imaginary realm.

There is much more that we could explore regarding Lacan's re-interpretation of the Oedipal crisis, but I do not believe that would be helpful at this juncture. However, I think that we delve a little deeper into Lacan's metapsychology of the subject more carefully we can gain an understanding of why his theory is valuable in growing as a mediator. Lacan attacks the idea of an essentialist subject that is transparent to itself and fully representable in theoretical discourse. It is this Cartesian subject which is also the subject of the humanist tradition that Lacan calls into question, as Freud did. This is to say that the cogito—that self reference that allows us to experience parts of life with clearness and distinctness— is a mirage—an illusion.[69] This move that reduces subjectivity to the conscious ego is a myth, according to Lacan. Thus, humans lose their center, as well as their autonomy; freedom is fragmented and delusional.

For Lacan, the essence of man is not to be found in his conscious representation of himself. In fact, the subject is not a psychological substratum that can be reduced to its own representation. If, indeed, there is an essence in the Lacanian subject it is as a lack of essence.

Nevertheless, his subject is different from the traditional metaphysical notion of the subject that is at the heart of the cogito. Thus the self is radically ex-centric to itself, heteronomous rather than autonomous, and more attached to the other than to itself. Thus the ego is different from the subject and is full of sedimentation of idealized images that are internalized during the mirror stage, which I explained above. Yet, there is always a gap between the imaginary ego and the lived experience of one's body, beginning in infancy. This gap shows us that the ego is always an alter ego constructed around a center that comes from the other—the other that gives one a sense of unity.

Any imaginary unity based on the mirror stage is therefore founded on an irreducible gap, between each human and his own image. Unity in the Imaginary is a result of captivation, of a power relation between the infant and its image. This captivation, which anticipates unity and synthesis, does not eliminate the alienating character of its own foundation. Thus, we attempt to identify with anything outside (of ourselves in order to recover the lost unity. Yet, what seems to be ours always contains an element of difference and alienation. It is because the imaginary image of ourselves does not give us a stable identity that we seek it out in the symbolic register, through language. We are not speaking chronologically here, but logically, in that the symbolic always presupposes the imaginary and even pre-exists as a network of anticipated meanings even before birth. Thus, even though the ego is formed in the Imaginary, the subject emerges [and is assimilated by] the Symbolic. The subject is thereby constituted by the signifier, which implies the loss of some possibilities and an entrance into the Symbolic, subordinated to those to which it is attached through mechanics of power.

The signifier is the epicenter of power that forms the subject and is based on the recognition of difference as well as a certain order. It is psychoanalysis that is the science of the signifier, as applied to the formation of subjectivity. Furthermore, for Lacan, psychoanalysis could be the new methodology that effects a reversal of the priority of the natural-empirical sciences over the human sciences. For him, modern physics and mathematics introduces measurement into the Real, and operates at one end of a dialectical process about scientific methodology. In sum, Lacan reconstructs Freud in terms of linguistics, thereby allowing him to go beyond the axiom that self is substance and reinterpreting it [the self] nominalistically.

What is important in this account for mediation is that the parties always talk in encoded ways that are based upon these illusions of subjectivity (and resulting life narrative structure). Fortunately, these encodings or ciphers can be understood through an analysis of the discourse each party uses. This may add another dimension to a structural-linguistic analysis and will be part of a much larger treatise that will include a careful account of discourse analysis. It is similar to Foucault in that it rightly understands the profound importance of language in power, and additionally valuable because it focuses on one's life history. In another work, I carefully delineate the difference between the part of ourselves that has transcendental freedom to make new choices (thus contributing to a cooperative mediation process) and another part of ourselves that is largely determined by old structure (and which precludes use from such change. It remains to be seen how we can construct a mediation environment that is sensitive to this understanding. In the next chapter, I will explore the difference between that part of us that is structurally sedimented and another part which is capable of transformation. It is this part that is that contributes to a cooperative, non-zero-sum dynamic that leads to mediation success.

X:
Beginnings of an Integration of the 3 Models

Now that we have taken an introductory look at the three models for new approaches to mediation, we can begin to integrate these views into a set of considerations that can later be converted into practice techniques. Let's start with a comparison of Lacan [the classical structuralist view] and Sartre [the existential-phenomenological view].

Lacan agrees with Sartre that the ego is an object, not a subject, of experience, and that therapeutic attempts to develop ego structure are misguided. In contrast to Sartre's belief that humans can transform their behavior and attitudes into more authentic experience, Lacan believes the best we can do is accept that we are determined by the linguistic unconscious. For Sartre, we discover ourselves as objects of others, but because of the pre-reflective aspect of consciousness we can overcome this. In contrast, for Lacan we literally take the other for ourselves and we can never overcome this fundamental alienation. Further, as I have shown, Lacan is a structuralist and believes that language "speaks" the person; it speaks through us and constitutes who we are. Thus he is also a reductionist who is searching for a scientific explanation for psychic phenomena that is experience distant and not experience near. In contrast to Freud, who discovers this in our biology, Lacan finds this in structural linguistics. Sartre, of course, objects to Lacan's determinism because it prevents the possibility of free and authentic action of individuals. This illuminates Sartre's prioritization of consciousness over Lacan's postulate of the structural unconscious. One fundamental question concerns the degree to which we can become self-aware. This is very important for a mediator who is engaged in a transformative and facilitative mediation.

However, there is some agreement between the two. Sartre would agree with Lacan's belief that the ego is an object that is more often an object of misunderstanding. Lacan echoes Sartre when he compares the subject to a paralytic who has been hypnotized by his image in a mirror—the ego. Sartre had similarly described the ego as a false representation of itself with which consciousness has hypnotized itself. Sartre's subject is stultified by the image of a substantial self whereas Lacan's subject is hypnotized by the substitution for a self of its own mirror image, and both agree that the rigidity of the ego must be questioned. Derivatively, both thinkers criticize psychoanalytic attempts to build ego structure, given that the ego is illusory for them.

Even so, for Sartre, the therapeutic [and awareness-building] enterprise would involve building a new reflective relationship with the ego; for Lacan, the ego is a fundamental alienation that can be acknowledged but not overcome. For him, even though human conflicts may appear on the horizon of the experience of the gaze, their actual origin is not the desire to co-opt the Other as a mirror for me as an object. Instead, their origin comes from the desire to mimic the Other and gain a self. Thus, Lacan rejects Sartre's fundamental ontology. For Lacan, both the self and the Other are objects, never subjects, which prevents the kind of positive social transformation that is possible within Sartre's ontology, in terms of viewing both the self and others as subjects that are deserving of respect. In Lacan's metapsychology, we all are objects merely trying to capture an image of wholeness by means of which the Other originally captured what might have been a self. In fact, the Lacanian ego is otherness absolutely and completely, and this means that there is no transcendent consciousness that can reflectively alter or develop the ego.

In contrast, for Sartre, we can purify the ego by understanding that we are never trapped or determined by it. Here, we give up false hope of attaining a substantialization of the self by understanding that the ego is only an effect and not a cause. In this process, we would understand that the ego is just a story that we tell about ourselves and that this story can be changed as we re-interpret our memories of the past. There are two parts of the ego for Sartre. There are the judgments of others and a reflective ipseity that allows us to accept or reject those judgments of others. This reflective capacity could allow for a radical conversion to a philosophy of freedom that promotes authentic relations with others.[70]

As a structuralist, Lacan tries to reduce psychic phenomena to unconscious linguistic structures by removing human intentionality and meaning. By reducing the conscious subject to an effect of the signifier, Lacan precludes meaningful transformation. His structuralism — which is a new positivism — has moved from a determinism based on historical causation to a determinism based on unconscious structural causation. Both forms of determinism are manifestations of an analytical reductionism that misses out on the power of Sartre's idea of intentional praxis. For Lacan, we are just playthings of the linguistic unconscious, which prevents us from using language as praxis. The implication is that we cannot alter the Symbolic Order, which in Sartre's vernacular renders us inert. That is, for Lacan there is no transcendent subject who can make such change.[71]

Even though Sartre also believes that language inscribes the Other into the heart of each person's being, he thinks that we have freedom in how we live that otherness. Such otherness is unconscious in the sense that it is not usually examined, but it is not unconscious in the sense of being beyond consciousness. There is a continuum of sorts between living ourselves in language as hexis or praxis.[72] Lacan's position, what Sartre would call hexis, is that language speaks us. As such, we are inert objects that are pure otherness and there is no chance for transcendence. As an inert repository of past praxes, language is always an invitation to hexis. Using language inserts us into a cultural order and, as a consequence of this, Otherness inscribes itself into our own intentional projects. Thus, for Lacan, otherness is at the very core of intentionality and "voluntary" deliberation.

In contrast, Sartre believes that we can live language as praxis, creatively and with a kind of intentionality that is self-constituting and self-originating.[73] It is this creative aspect of language that Lacan perhaps avoids. By neglecting intentionality and denigrating consciousness, Lacan's position becomes very close to the one Sartre ascribes to Flaubert. By placing the source of otherness inside the linguistic unconscious, Lacan considers normal the kind of alienation Sartre describes in his concept of hexis. Lacanian alienation is unsurpassable because it is solely this Otherness that has created me as a speaking subject. For Lacan we always enter into a world that is filled with symbols, and we can never return to a place that is outside the cultural-linguistic order. Theoretically, Lacan converts intentionality [as constituting consciousness] into a mode of perception [amongst others] that negotiates desire through object substitutions. It is also true that awareness of desire is at the same time a desire for recognition:

perhaps one is the alias for the other. It is there in the repressed primal relationship with the mother and in the linguistic laws that that have been placed there after the encounter with the primal signifier that the various substitutions one uses makes sense. For Lacan, the most one an do is to understand that we are the mercy of the linguistic unconscious, that one is a signified rather than a signifier, an object pretending to be a subject. Sartre, on the other hand, believes that we can use language in a way that transcends the Lacanian position.

We must also explore the possibilities for reconciling Lacan's structuralist position with Sartre's phenomenological approach by utilizing Foucault's ideas (as mentioned) about the nature of the subject. Again, we are trying to uncover some aspect of the self that can escape from the objectifying categories of contemporary psychology. This is, perhaps not equivalent to Sartre's idea of transcendence, but it may enjoy similar consequences. Lacanian analysis is not ego analysis but instead is discourse analysis, in which we try to understand how conscious discourse emerges from its unconscious source. Recall that Lacan absolutely rejects the attempt by ego psychologists and object-relations theorists to reconstruct the development of the ego. For him, these approaches are an unproductive rendering of Freud in that they are directed by the false ideal of "normal" development, a concept that Foucault attacks.

Lacanian analysis focuses on understanding the illusory nature of the ego in the interest of a fuller experience of subjectivity that subsists beyond the phallic signifier. This, Lacan argues that attempts to shore up or reconstruct the ego result in a reinforced sort of alienation because these theorists do not understand that the go is an illusion—a fiction. Instead of being a force for reality organization, the ego is a collective force—a name—for all the resistances to the treatment of symptoms. This occurs because the ego is organized around the specular images that give the individual a sense of imaginary coherence based on identification. Therefore, ego analysis takes place in the Imaginary register and, in opposition, Lacan believes that effective analysis and self-understanding occurs in the corridor between the symbolic and the imaginary.

Instead of restructuring the ego, Lacan advocates the reconstruction of the signifying chain by which a person has been constructed.[74] The goal is full or true speech that occurs without the disrupting intervention of ego identifications. Full speech differs from empty speech in that it realizes the truth that subjectivity is an illusion. In empty speech the subject loses "himself" in the systems and structures of language that are based on cultural claims to truth and value, forced into the status quo by relations of power and governmentalization.

This dialectic is important for understanding mediation because it highlights the limitations of autonomy; at the very least it is a criticism of the belief that we are fully autonomous. If this is so, then one of the core tenets of a full and true mediation process is put into question. If we are structurally determined in ways that we do not understand, then those who direct the mediation (the mediator, the lawyers, and perhaps the courts) are actually in charge (in an unconscious way); what looks like choices and negotiation between the parties might already be pre-ordained by the mediation (relational) structure itself. On the other hand, if subjectivity always includes elements of autonomy and free choice then we can rightly make (and honor) the choices of the participants as part of a constructive and productive process. There is more work that must be done on this very point.

XI:
Accomplice Recruiting (Wachtel) & Sado-Masochism (Sartre)

In earlier chapters, I made preliminary comments about a psychoanalytic approach to mediation and other cooperative/collaborative conflict resolution processes. I am particularly interested in the unconscious and less-than-conscious processes that occur between professional, third party "neutrals" and their clients. I am especially interested in how these processes can distort idealized versions of neutrality and ultimately how professionals can take corrective action, introspectively. I also delineated three separate approaches, one from Existential Psychoanalysis, one from Classical Psychoanalysis, and one from linguistic-structuralism (which deposits itself in a sort of discourse analysis). Here, I'd like to make a few comments about the work of a leading existentialist and a leading psychoanalyst. Let's discuss the ideas of both Paul Wachtel, who is a psychoanalyst, especially his notion of accomplice recruiting, and Jean-Paul Sartre's ideas about sado-masochistic relational dynamics that he writes about in "Concrete Relations," in his major existential treatise, Being and Nothingness.

Wachtel writes: "the cyclical psychodynamic formulation refers to the patient's entire way of life. It points to how all of the patient's experiences must be understood in their relational context." What he is saying is dangerously close to what an existential analyst would proffer, that each of us is grounded in a basic orientation to the world that colors all social interactions. In the technical jargon, this is the language of ontology (made popular by both Heidegger and Sartre). Furthermore, Wachtel asserts that all of our relationships, past and current, affect in a fluid way, any present social interaction.[75] Thus, in contrast to the relational theorists, Wachtel thinks we need to look at a person's current social constellation, as well as those in the past, in order to create a practical analytic system/method for understanding that person's relational proclivities and possibilities in any new encounter. A derivative of this theory (for a classical theorist) is that humans unconsciously "recruit" others as accomplices in the perpetuation of our [usually not so healthy] life patterns. This is to say that our inner world is constructed externally, conjointly with others. Wachtel himself also believes that critical awareness of these patterns can help change them into more healthy ones; this also implies that we stop recruiting accomplices, especially in inappropriate environments.

If we value Wachtel's assumptions, we can see how the understanding of our active relational matrix informs all of our social interactions. For a professional mediator or conflict resolution specialist, this sort of knowledge and understanding seems indispensable to excellent work and an ethical footing. Unfortunately, a lack of this understanding can lead to distorted mediations that are not so neutral and not so fair. If we are unaware of how pieces of our relational matrix are triggered in different ways by different clients, then we would be unaware of how our semiological constructions, i.e., word choice, inflections, and nonverbal communications, profoundly affect the process. Now let's turn to Sartre, the existentialist.

Sartre did not believe in the unconscious; he did, however, believe that we are ineluctably drawn to self-deceptive constructions of reality that allow us to relax from full ownership of our free choices. These sedimentations hold true perspectives about reality in place and can usually only be reconstituted through analytic and therapeutic processes or, for some, through rigorous self-examination. Yet, they operate very much like the dynamic unconscious does for a classical theorist such as Wachtel. Moreover, Wachtel's insight that relational matrices together operate as a whole self—that they point to an entire way of life—is a belief that the existentialists came to a century ago.

As I have started to outline in earlier chapters of this theoretical inquiry, each of us has a foundational orientation toward the world, such choice being made at an early age, but one that acts as bedrock for all other choices in value and action. In his famous, Being and Nothingness ("BN"), Sartre pens a particularly brilliant section entitled "Concrete Relations," in which he outlines the very process Wachtel refers to by which we unwittingly seek "accomplices." For Sartre, we constantly seek out social relations, in various degrees, that tend to minimize the pure realization of our absolute freedom of interpretation of the world. This is not to say that we are absolutely free in a practical sense, but it is to assert that at an ontological level, i.e., how we interpret experience, that we do have radical freedom. Sartre discusses these processes in terms of a complex psychological dynamic between sadistic and masochistic elements in all of us. Thus, a sadistic choice extinguishes the freedom of another and therefore closes relational [and self] growth; a masochistic choice allows the freedom of another to dictate action and this extinguishes the masochist's freedom [and the freedom of the other which, paradoxically, engages the inertness of the masochist]. It is a complicated section, but I believe is the most analytically sophisticated account heretofore.[76]

In most family law mediation and in some business/transactional mediation, there are deep ontological dynamics at play; in some cases of business mediation these dynamics are present but play a much smaller role; this is the case, because there is less emotional investment in the relationships at play. However, this is not to say that we are ever free from them. The key to facilitating successful mediation is to recognize how the conflict of gazes — a dualistic metaphysics — creates an inflexible, win-lose system. Mediations that are based on this dynamic are rarely sustainable, let alone completed; this is why we must transform them into win-win (mutual benefit agreement), non-zero-sum processes in which both parties are fulfilled.

Most dyads that come to mediation — especially in divorce or partnership dissolution — live in accord with a sado-masochistic dynamic. This is the social dimension of a deeper ontological need to create a substantial self, one that is like other objects in the world; one that attempts to create complete coincidence between one's actuality and one's possibilities.[77] In short, because of the radical nature of human possibility, we become frightened and try to delimit these possibilities by engaging in bad faith strategies that hide this level of freedom. We do this through ideas, money, places, jobs, and most importantly, relationships, in either a sadistic or a masochistic mode. Mediation can actually reverse this process by facilitating a mutual good faith enterprise that values the freedom of each participant equally.[78]

Let's look more deeply. Two main ways that we attempt to avoid our freedom involve sadism or masochism. In sadism, I try to manipulate the other into submerging himself into me. In masochism, I try to submerge myself into the consciousness of the other. Individuals often come to mediation with a complex version of these dynamics, especially in family law divorce. It is also often the case that these orientations form a circle: each is unstable and contains within it the other as opposite. What we also see is that each person in the dyad holds both the sadistic and masochistic sides; the relationship plays them out. A simple way of seeing these dynamics is that in a competitive, adversarial dyad, there is a conflict of gazes/looks in such a way that both attempt to dominate [or in the masochistic mode, be dominated]. In this competitive mode, two selves cannot approach their dyad with mutuality and reciprocity, allowing their dyad to hold both subjectivities simultaneously: in this model, one subjective (self) requires an objective (self). Without the other I lose the means to found my objective being. Also, if I try to recover that objective being by identifying with the other's freedom as its foundation, I learn that the separation of consciousnesses prevents me from doing so. The other always remains an alien freedom that I can never absorb; in addition, I remain a freedom without substantive being. In short, there is always ontological separation between two people, and each always has ontological freedom to choose new interpretations and behaviors.

In my experience, this S-M model of dyadic interaction is very helpful in mediation, especially in family or divorce law. The parties—which I often refer to as "conflict partners"—enter the mediation process with their own blueprint of sado-masochistic dynamics. Even though there are usually several complex levels, there is often a basic S-M appearance: for example, one spouse can appear in the role of sadist, the other as masochist. This provides the mediator with a starting point in the facilitation toward freedom, which we should explore now to some extent. By substituting out these ontological sedimentations and replacing them with a pact toward the mutual promotion of freedom conflict can transform from zero-sum structures to non-zero-sum alliances. This implies a rejection of attempts to coerce, manipulate, or degrade the other, and a valorization of the promotion of the freedom of the other as one promotes his own. By letting go of these ontological entanglements we curtail our desires to use the other as a bad faith attempt to create self-coincidence in consciousness, one that attempts co-extensivity between actuality and possibility. In this new dynamic for a mediating dyad, both individuals exchange their competing gazes and attempts toward sado-masochistic dynamics for a reciprocal exchange in which both parties simultaneously respect each other as autonomous subjects, participating in mediation in a positive and constructive way. This involves honesty, transparency, acceptance of the other's goals, and empathy.

Both Sartre and Wachtel arrive at similar conclusions about the genesis and development of distortions in social interaction even though they utilize very different theoretical machinery with different assumptions and different theories of mind. For our purposes, however, each approach shows us the dangers of not becoming aware of these relational matrices in us that are unwittingly activated in different ways by different people at different times. A professional mediator ought to consider these conclusions and adopt them as a part of a professional program for ethical and practical awareness.

XII:
Beginnings of Praxis:
Before & During the
Meeting

In previous chapters, I started to delineate the psychoanalytic considerations in mediation. It is my goal to raise preliminary considerations for all three models. To that end, in this chapter I will delineate further considerations that are relevant for all the models, as follows:

In contrast to Descartes, who believed that we could know objective truths about the world by meeting the standard of clearness and distinctness (in consciousness), the existential psychoanalytic approach (hereinafter "EP," which utilizes phenomenology) challenges us to focus on the immediate givens of conscious experience and interrogate them in order to obtain a fuller, richer ability to meet the world and especially to meet other humans relationally—with greater perspicacity and understanding. In this chapter, I'd like to address some of the considerations a mediator might consider on his or her way to a client meeting.

The existentialists have shown through rigorous theorizing that our simple, native immediate consciousness is merely the starting point in reflecting about all the complex processes going on in ourselves at any point in time. We can, however, probe into that immediate awareness in a way that creates a much more attentive and focused professional interaction. For example, we always live within the physical, social, personal, and spiritual dimensions. As such, I can ask myself about my physical and material world. Is my body tired? What are the road conditions? What sort of route did I decide to take to the meeting? Instead, of experiencing consciousness in a purely reactive mode, which so many do, we can actually move into a reflective state and dialogue with ourselves about how we are experiencing the material world. The reason is simple: How we relate to our environment creates an interpretive mood from which we orient ourselves professionally. Without asking these questions, we end up going into a professional setting blindly and emotionally, perhaps missing vital clues from our communication with our clients.

Second, we should also interrogate ourselves about how we are relating socially at the time. What were my interactions like the night before? This morning? Were there any particularly challenging or distressing social interactions that could significantly affect my mood? In which way could they? On the road, did anyone cut me off, or did other drivers seem friendly and generous? Again, I can ask these sorts of questions to develop an immediate sense of my constellation of moods, which includes some assumptions about our meeting. This can also provide clues about our propensities for reactivity should unexpected conflict ensue. At a deeper level, this allows us to begin to unravel the complex set of intentionalities with which we are meeting the day and ultimately, our clients.

Third, I must carefully ask myself about my own personal dimension, which is a derivative and reflective mode that usually emerges from thoughts about recent (and distant) social interactions. We each take a point of view on ourselves, which we cannot help. Furthermore, this point of view greatly colors our cognitive assumptions about upcoming social interactions. For example, if I made a mistake yesterday, I might be highly critical of myself today and therefore I might be somewhat paranoid or highly critical of self (and others), thereby distorting a more balanced view of upcoming social phenomena. We always experience anxiety about the future, i.e., the sheer uncertainty about how events will go, and we can interpret this anxiety in a number of ways. How we view ourselves as well as mediate the moods within we presence ourselves has a profound effect on how we relate to others socially.

Finally, when I am in a reflective mode, I often consider the meaning of recent events, which in existential terms, triggers consideration of the spiritual dimension. This can work in both directions: the meaning that I assign to previous experience can paralyze my ability to assimilate new social experience, or it can de-sediment it and unlock a more flexible range of interpretation. This meaning-giving process is the very way we grow both personally and professionally. Further considerations include time, anxiety, and "facts" we know about our clients. Let me suggest a few ideas about these very important aspects of human experience.

We always live in time and we always make interpretations of our temporality. This is how it comes to be that we sometimes experience time as moving fast and other times moving slowly, and so forth. In my experience, it is wise to consider how I am interpreting time, for this greatly affects how I experience communication flow, meeting protocols, objectives, and nonverbal communication. My anxiety is just how I live my uncertainty, and for mediators, I believe it is crucial to create heightened awareness about this uncertainty. All too often, we end up in our imagination/memory, when we should be in our immediate present experience meeting the requirements of the moment.

These are some basic considerations from the perspective of EP (Model A). There are many more to follow, as well as their relationship to unconscious processes, if one accepts such a theory of mind. In future work, I will address important existential elements of professional meetings, including ideas about heightening one's professional awareness and use of language, both verbal and nonverbal. It is still my belief the notion of a "neutral" mediator (or any neutral third) is suspect, falsely resting on a modernist anthropology of human being-ness that no longer is convincing, as well as a social ontology that must be refined for greater accuracy and practical use value.

Now that we have delineated some considerations that mediation professionals could reflect on prior to a meeting, we can focus on the meeting itself. This will add more practical content to the ongoing discussion regarding the existential psychoanalytic approach to mediation and collaborative law.

First, we can reflect on how the mediation clients actually get to your office, as well as your own trip to the meeting. Is it a long trip? Is traffic congested? Did the client have to negotiate with another family member to set the meeting? What is the weather like? What time of day and which day of the week is the meeting? I have found that these considerations are of significance because they affect the basic assumptions and mood of the meeting. Try as we might to contrive a Cartesian position (subject as originator of meaning), there is actually a universe of forces, considerations, and demands operating just below the surface of immediate awareness. In my experience, these considerations affect a professional meeting as much or more than what seems most immediate in consciousness. Let's be clear, however, that we can make these other considerations, including mood, part of an immediate awareness once we bring them into full awareness.

Second, initial greetings, including the location and environment of the office, are crucial to establishing a foundation upon which a meeting is built. Phenomenology, which we have discussed in a very introductory way in earlier segments, can help us in this regard. As such, we could ask the following questions: Is there a parking garage? Does it cost money? Is it easy and convenient for a client to make it to the office from the garage? Is your office clearly marked in the lobby? Do you have a receptionist? How does that person interface with new clients? What sort of mood is he or she in? After the client gets past the receptionist, how do you initially greet him or her? Do you approach first, in an assertive way, or allow the client come to you? Does it matter? Do you offer a handshake? Do you offer a beverage? Once inside your private office, do you spend time checking in with the client about her assumptions, mood, time availability, and considerations you think are relevant, or do you go straight into the substance of the meeting? In short, every single factor involved in a mediation process contributes substantially to the overall range of existential moods, dynamics, and relations that can emerge from the process. Phenomenology requires us to disabuse ourselves of sedimented beliefs and theories about how things ought to go, or unthinking ways that we devise our processes. Instead, it asks us to carefully scrutinize the existential elements as I have outlined. Let's continue.

If there is more than one client, how do you handle it? If it is a collaborative process with several professionals and at least two clients, how do you greet everyone? Does it matter? What sort of message do you send? Do you notice the client's nonverbal cues? What sorts of feeling does the initial greeting engender in you? What do you suppose is occurring for the client during your experience? If you notice a strong feeling in the client, do you consider shifting your own nonverbal or verbal behavior? These are just a few of the many existentially oriented questions we can ask in such circumstances. When there are additional clients or professionals, these dynamics become even more complex but should be dealt with in the same way. This will enable a mediator to create the most efficacious mediation or collaborative environment possible.

After the initial greetings (assuming at least two mediation clients), we must consider what happens next. I want to reiterate that at this point, most professionals follow some sort of tried-and-true protocol that follows community and personal practice guidelines. However, it is also very important to reflect on one's own immediate process, which concerns feelings, cognitions, and perceptions. If a mediator does not do that then she eventually becomes de-humanized and mechanized in her process and, I believe, much less effective in her or his role. By checking in with ourselves we can become more immediately aware of what existential footing we are bringing into the mediation or collaboration. In my opinion, this is a crucial and essential element in competent and ethically sensitive professional practice. More importantly, it is necessary to think about the sorts of feelings and moods that presence themselves during these initial interactions. Why? These early dynamics always set the tone of any professional meeting and greatly influence communicative processes, including diction, inflection, tempo, and other subtle factors. Thus, merely following rules and clarifying goals is never sufficient but always necessary. The psychoanalytic approach to mediation — using any of the three approaches I have outlined earlier — requires more. When I develop this text into a much longer work, I will add more analysis concerning the unconscious and more analysis about linguistic structure.

Third, it is important to quickly become aware of the sorts of narrative structures and choice of metaphors that the parties use, even in their greetings and in initial small talk. What we will learn later in the development of these psychoanalytic models — existential, classical, and linguistic — is that words almost always are codifications of more basic internal and relational struggles. So while it is always important to think about how clients talk, it is equally important to consider what we say and what they say. By understanding initial metaphors we have an immediate access to a client's own existential orientation on that day at that time, as well as how he or she constructs meaning relative to the conflict situation and to the conflict partner. When I say that words are almost always codifications, I mean that there a number of dynamic levels of the construction meaning occurring at any one time. What gets said is often just a choice that is mediated by the immediate situation, often viewed as the best way to alleviate anxiety. By viewing what is said — what is presenced — as a dynamic choice relative to what is not said or what could have been said, we can begin to understand our clients to a much deeper level. Let me remind us that we are still focused on the existential level, which is constructed with the assumption that there is not an unconscious, but that there are degrees of awareness. If we assume a metaphor or the mind that includes an unconscious we can explore these very same issues with this new assumption. It is also true that we must approach an analysis of the unconscious carefully, for if there really is a dynamic unconscious, which we may or may not become aware of even with acute reflection. Let's continue for now with the existential approach.

With regard to self-examination and the examination of the statements of the disputing parties, some of the questions we can ask about these early statements are as follows: How did a statement express a relational element? Did it include you, the professional, or was it just about a conflict partner? Where did the client position herself in those relations? Who was the focus of the client's concerns? What sort of role was suggested for you to play? What sorts of feelings and thoughts came up for you? There are many more questions to ask, but the main point is to focus on meta-textual reverberations of meaning that help identify how a client orients himself toward that conflict and what role the mediator is being asked to play.

Some consideration might be given to who talks first. The reason is that every single element of the initial greeting, communication (both verbal and nonverbal), and overall relational dynamic has a profound effect on the outcome of the conversation, mediation, or collaborative process. To say that a professional is ever neutral, in my opinion, is somewhat of a misnomer and most certainly is misleading. This is so because the sort of inter-relational process that is created determines the way that the professional conversation goes. At this point in our exploration, I want to keep this consideration simple, but as we delve deeper into the possibility of the dynamic unconscious we will see that this consideration is pivotal. Without an acute awareness of how this process works, a professional can unwittingly create an unconscious relational dynamic that can negatively distort the outcome of the professional meeting. Initially, however, we must consider the level just below that of immediate awareness.

I have found that an effective way to bring as much of this process to awareness is to immediately follow up with reference to any previous meetings or conversations. This always allows for a client to let you know right away how he or she is feeling and what his [conscious] assumptions are about the meeting at hand. Further, we can reflect on the client's narrative-right then and there—about what is happening—to gain a great deal of understanding about how to proceed most effectively. In my experience, how a client communicates is just as important as what she communicates substantively. Unfortunately, we don't pay attention to this process dimension enough and therefore lose vital clues about how to proceed with the greatest amount of awareness. This is not to say that the content is unimportant, for the story of the day is often a codified account of the client's basic assumptions, mood, and inter-relational posture to the professional [you.] It is essential therefore that the mediator listen carefully to the most-likely codifications in the client's [or clients'] account(s) of the what is happening.

With these initial considerations in mind for this early portion of a meeting we can ask the following questions: What was said? How was it expressed? What did you notice about the accompanying nonverbal body posture? What inter-relational elements were expressed toward you? About you? About the other parties? Any other professionals? How did the client position himself in those expressed relational dynamics? Did this reveal any basic existential concerns about self? Other? The situation as a whole? These are only a small portion of the possible sorts of relevant considerations and questions we could ask of ourselves—as professionals—in the early stage of any client meeting, but I think they are especially important to collaborative law and mediation processes. With greater awareness, we can focus attention more acutely and with greater accuracy, thereby becoming more proficient.

In future work, I will continue to explore underlying existential, psychoanalytic, and linguistic dynamics in professional meetings, including what I believe to be the most effective corrective to our own distortions, which is the phenomenological method that I summarized early in this text. It sets a fundamental ground for relational experience that can be used to develop intra-psychic language for a mediator and inter-relational language with clients.

Hopefully, I have opened up new sets of questions in each of the proposed three models for a new approach to mediation. My intent is to develop higher and more accurate standards of practice in mediation, and I believe that by putting into question our commitments to the underlying philosophies of mind and social ontologies that we use in the mediation environment, we can re-constitute the praxis of cooperative conflict resolution. My comments are exploratory and provisional, and I know that there is much more work that must be done. Some of what I have stated is underdeveloped; some of it may be wrong. Nevertheless, I write from my own clinical experience as a psychoanalyst, lawyer, and mediator; from conversations I have had with several colleagues; from my own previous research; from life. The reader should expect a much better thought out and more developed book from me on this subject in the future. My goal in writing this one was and is to motivate and propel others forward with collaborative research on mediation practice.

Endnotes

1.   Unfortunately, scientists, psychologists, and other professionals including mediators have been saddled with the phenomenological limitations of the so-called objective view. This has greatly constricted what we consider to be useful and legitimate data.

2.   It is my belief that we do not need "neutrality" in order to have fairness. The book not only spells this out; it also explains why we wouldn't choose it because there is a better approach. This is psychoanalysis.

3.   This involves the projection of one's own reality into one's interpretation of the "facts." More insidiously, this could involve projective identification, in which the unconscious of one or both parties can actually influence the thinking and behavior of the mediator. It is good to be aware of this phenomenon.

4.   I call this the "phenomenological field," something I will account for in great detail in one of the next books in our mediation series.

5.   I account for this in the existential psychoanalytic approach to mediation, which I dedicate much space to in this prolegomena.

6.   This requires a new philosophy (and metaphor) of mind.

7.   Ontology is the science of being, which is a holistic approach toward understanding how a person motivates and intends thoughts, emotions, and behavior.

8.   This implies that thought is structured by culture, society, and language.

9.   The idea is that we repress certain thoughts that are not acceptable to us, in the psychoanalytic model; in contrast, in the existential phenomenological, we engage in clever strategies of self-deception.

10.   I acknowledge that even this book is affected or structured by social and linguistic structural considerations. To what extent we can gain

perspective about them is an important theoretical debate that I take up elsewhere.

11. Descartes is largely responsible for shepherding the view that a subject can become certain of an objective world if he follows the correct methodology. It is this view that I challenge in this book. Phenomenology challenges this view, as I carefully explain here.

12. Much of psychology and psychoanalysis now acknowledges and in some cases, valorizes the use of relatedness as a theoretical paradigm. In this book, the read will see its center role in sado-masochism, cyclical dynamics, and object relations psychoanalysis. It has replaced the old Freudian drive theory as a leading model of explaining psychic phenomena. Atomic individualism is an old view of the self that has been largely discarded; at the least, it is not used as much to explain inter-relational phenomena, certainly not in dyadic and triadic professional contexts.

13. We each have a kind of "Kantian" filter that is situated at the very core of our perception and understanding, which affects (and distorts) our judgments about mediation phenomena. Whereas Kant examined universal features of this filter (for example, space and time), I am more interested in how each person's personal history creates a baseline of assumptions about other people, oneself, mediation, conflict, and how the world works in general. By exploring these filters, I believe that a mediator can minimize distortions in perception and judgment, as well as work with the ones s/he has.

14. I believe that we need the most accurate paradigm of the self that is possible in order to re-construct more powerful and effective mediation theory and practice. A you read through this text you will see different views about the nature of the self and how they lead to different professional practice.

15. Unfortunately, this all to often leads to narcissistic and distorted judgments about conflict, which can be challenging to overcome in the resolution process.

16. This leads to a conception of mediation that is full of best practices and techniques but which lacks understanding and creative problem

solving. Good mediation practice is more than mathematical optimization; it involves intuition, empathy, and a sensitivity to how the parties solve their relational differences especially when this involves understanding the irrationalities of the process.

17. This is an important skill to have in mediation. Senior mediators will often relay that the facts change, or more facts are added during the process that can change the resolution options and outcomes.

18. This is the narcissistic self that often plays a zero-sum game out of fear and anxiety. Good mediation process can partially overcome this position in consciousness as a way to create more rationality, empathy, and a non-zero-sum game, which can lead to more possibilities for resolution.

19. Although it is helpful for mediating parties to look to the future, we also want to encourage them to look into the present, especially at the ways in which they approach the situation and how they treat their conflict partners. This can help avoid obsessional processes that are based on anxiety, as well as open new options and outcomes.

20. Reflexivity is encouraged in mediation, but can be difficult because of the stressful situations with which most mediating parties are faced. By leading the parties from the fight or flight response of the instinctual limbic brain stem toward the higher functioning processes of the cerebral cortex, a good mediator can increase the probabilities of a successful and sustainable result.

21. It is my argument that we are not as aware of ourselves as we might naively think, unless we engage in radical reflection in one of the ways I outline in this text (or other ways) as a way to overcome the distortions of the daily ego. In a professional context such as mediation, this goal is important if not crucial. In any event, if we think in this way we can overcome the hubris associated with focusing solely on the parties and not the mediator himself.

22. In mediation, we see all too often how people can be irrational and chaotic, oscillating between cooperation and competition as they became both receptive and defensive at the same time. Our research institute is engaged in mathematical and psychoanalytic research

regarding this oscillation. The point, however, is that there is not just one static self. Instead, there is a complex self process that is multiple, variable, and sometimes unpredictable.

23. One of the main ethical points I argue for in mediation is that the mediator has a duty to facilitate the restoration of the fullest autonomy in each conflict partner. This allows each to make the most rational choice and best decision for him or her. This obviously requires mediators to have skill, education, and experience, and a willingness to take a perspicacious look in the mirror.

24. Under Kant's moral theory, individuals respect the autonomy of the other by choosing universalizable maxims of behavior that treat each human as a moral end in itself. That is, in highly sustainable mediation, the mediator facilitates a mutual outcome that achieves this goal to some extent. I will explore these moral proscriptions in more detail in another work.

25. By the way, it is often egocentrism that mediators have to "combat" in their facilitation to non-zero-sum game dynamics. This requires experience and a highly proactive approach, including the sharing of a "Prisoner's Dilemma" sort of analysis with the conflict partners. Even selfish, egocentric clients like best outcomes; sometimes this requires giving a little in order to get more in the end.

26. A philosophy of mind just means the sort of metaphor, picture, or blueprint of the self that is foundation to understandings about the self. It may include structural, topographical, or dynamic elements as a part of it construction.

27. One can see how the Archimedean point shifts in such a way that the world becomes bigger as a human's ability to understand it becomes correlatively smaller.

28. Sometimes we see one client acting more as an isolated individualist (with practical agreements made with the other party) and the other client acting more relationally even as they diverge and leave each other. This sometimes cuts along gender lines.

29. This split between the honest self and the potentially duplicitous self can be understood through psychoanalysis, game theory, nonverbal communication, and additional theories and discourses. It helps

with need-based analysis as well as with the understanding of unconscious processes and phenomena.

30. This is the sort of self that we have inherited from the Enlightenment and against which we must struggle. All too many times, our hubris as professionals can lead us to false conclusions and less than competent practice. It is my belief that by humbling ourselves through the recognition of an unconscious, we can approach our cases with more prudence and care than we otherwise might.

31. Metapsychology has changed since Freud: from drive theory to either relationships or language as primary metaphor/domain. We are currently striving toward better paradigms that capture a fuller and more accurate range of phenomena of human experience. The more phenomena that we can account for the more accurate and trenchant our understandings of a mediation encounter will be.

32. By understanding both conscious and unconscious intentionalities of the disputing parties, a mediator will then have a rich, deep, and helpful understanding of what is at stake for each of them. This helps a mediator facilitate fully autonomous and rational decisions on the part of each party.

33. Sometimes unresolved impulses show up in mediation, especially because divorce can trigger regression and the opening of older, repressed memories and issues. We currently have a research program in gender issues that explores this idea. One simple technique is for the mediator to speak in ways that clearly differentiates the present divorce situation from any issues in one's personal history or childhood.

34. Mediators can empower themselves if they accept that they need to try to decipher what their clients are saying to them, and if they engage in deconstructive processes to understand their own struggles, issues, interpretations, and encodings. To the extent that we don't do this we mishandle our mediations. Unconscious issues create aggression, which can be used for destructive purposes or positive and constructive purposes. Freud's drive theory helps to explain aggression.

35. The self that clients present is just the tip of the iceberg, the result of this Freudian-explained compromise.

36. It is difficult to gain perspective because we are already so embedded within language. Finding a transcendental position from which we can make claims that even remotely approach objectivity is very difficult. This leads to sound practice, which involves the sharing of perspective and experience but not necessarily wisdom.

37. This is our hubris, and it works against us in mediation encounters. We are learning the importance of staying open and vigilant to the "new," by which we are always humbled.

38. By rejecting this view we can honestly express ourselves to our mediation clients without claiming what is best, right, or true. This does not obviate the need to share obvious legal, procedural, substantive, and other relevant matters, including a game theory analysis of the case.

39. We argue that proactive mediation that is dynamically rich, inquisitive, dialectically active, and open in a forward-moving way tends toward better results.

40. It is important to facilitate this shift in consciousness in the very early stages of the mediation process, for it sets a productive tone and structural-linguistic elements that are positive in nature and which allow for the greatest possible cooperation.

41. Setting very clear housekeeping rules and expectations creates safety, alleviates anxiety, and fosters trust in the mediation process and in the mediator.

42. Writing a well-drafted agreement with specificity and careful detail extends the safe container of the mediation process into a memorialized, mutual statement of expectation and intention. I have found that this document can signify more than the words themselves; it can evoke a deep commitment to its provisions.

43. I have found that it is very difficult for some individuals to consider that the unconscious has powerful intentionalities and motivations that we have a difficult time becoming aware of; it can feel distressing for a professional to realize that s/he is not as aware of the situation as s/he formerly believed. This is not to say, however,

that professionals cannot become more aware if they acknowledge these processes.

44. In the early education phase of mediation, a good mediator can explain to the clients the sorts of experience that they can expect, including difficult to discern unconscious processes. This can open up both the clients and the mediator to a vulnerable making honesty, which always translates into a more accurate and sustainable resolution.

45. Instead, I think we can understand these dynamics and work with them relative to standards of fairness, sustainability, and full autonomy.

46. This is so because we can enter into dialogue with ourselves and with our clients. This dialogue is more important, helpful, and fertile than you might think, for it opens a transcendental space that can ultimately allow for greater perspective and more degrees of freedom. This creates more options for resolution.

47. This is one of the main tenets of "postmodernism," a historically based term that expresses shifts in assumptions about progress, knowledge, the self, social relations, and the like.

48. There are very complicated mathematical dynamics that express the oscillation between playing a zero-sum game and a non-zero-sum game. Frequently, evaluative mediation is a zero-sum, competitive game (sometimes called "hardball" negotiation), whereas cooperative (facilitative) mediation involves both types of games but leans toward the non-zero-sum. This book is focused on facilitative mediation.

49. There is an interesting psychological issue emerging from whether the parties are playing a game with an indefinite number of iterations or whether there is a finite set of iterations. For example, parties who have a common interest (co-parenting) may play the game differently (more cooperative leanings) than parties who do not have children and who will wrap up their mutual affairs in a final dissolution process. We are developing a greater understanding of this issue in our game theory research.

50. I have found it helpful to discuss my clients' attitudes toward

conflict with them before proceeding into the process. This is an integral part of the early educational process and consciousness shifting that maximizes both parties' readiness to step into the cooperative process.

51. The comparison between individualism and relationalism is complex, involving the ontology of our very conceptions of the self, dyads, small groups, and more. Individualism is a paradigm that the holds that the self is its own original foundation and then derivatively discovers the Other; in contrast, relationalism is a position that holds that a self does not emerge except as it is in relation to Others. For our discussion, an important point is that relationalism is a way to overcome the priority of rights; this opens up critical thinking space about cooperation that can overcome apparent conflict.

52. The goal in facilitative, transformative mediation is always to move beyond a rights-based, substantive approach while remaining sensitive to it. This keeps the parties in a reflective equilibrium.

53. In game theory, which I explore in our next book on mediation, we will see how the prospect of a continuing relationship with indefinite iterations can affect a willingness to move from zero-sum dynamics to non-zero-sum dynamics. In cases where the relationship will end on a specific date, this willingness is affected either by empathy or by extraneous factors such as how mutual friends, work associates, or the general community will regard each of the parties.

54. The topic of non-verbal communication is very important to becoming proficient in mediation. At our institute we have a research program in it, and are working on the beginnings of a mediation text.

55. This is part of the noetic aspect of directing our attention—by making an intention—to any object real or imagined. There are many ways we see things, and many features of knowing, such as mood, emotion, intuition, and the like that affect how we apprehend phenomena. In mediation it is important for a mediator to know how she is approaching the situation and what she is bringing into it.

56. This worldview analysis gives us useful information and vital

perspectives about how each of the participants approaches and solves conflict. It is also helpful for a mediator to perform such analysis on himself.

57. This is discourse analysis.

58. Cross-cultural communication is an important learning dimension of competent mediation.

59. I think it is important for a mediator to be in a consultation group with other mediators or a confidential group or individual psychotherapeutic process. Long-term work can bring one's issues to the surface, which creates the possibility of psychological change. This can dramatically affect the mediator's abilities.

60. Even though the drive theory has been largely replaced by various relational paradigms, it is still important scrutinize the specific ways that they avoid pain and pursue pleasure/satisfaction. This sort of data can also be obtained through existential phenomenological analysis even though the operational language is different.

61. Even though Sartre does not use the word "accomplice," he gives a penetrating and insightful view of how we make relationships as a way to work through our propensities to deal with anxiety. The analysis is ontological, and shows how we annihilate freedom (ours or our partner's) by dominating the other or allowing him/her to dominate our own subjectivity.

62. The multiple self doctrine.

63. Foucault wrote many books that are a type of critical history, examining how we create scientific and political discourses that are structuralized in terms of the relation between power and knowledge, explaining how the "true" and the "false" are articulated in various disciplines and historical epochs. He is especially interested in how power colonizes language, prefiguring the very way we engage in critical thinking. This is especially important to mediation theory and practice.

64. One could make the argument that the power dynamics of disputing parties follow them into mediation. It is up to the mediator to help facilitate their emergence in cooperative discourse, creating and developing a safe container that equalizes or neutralizes any power

dynamics that preclude fair resolution.

65. If we believe in this notion then we know that parties come into a mediation without full awareness of how their very subjectivities are already pre-figured by relations of power that invest in language. Without this awareness, it is more difficult to arrive at a mutual equilibrium that is optimal and that is fair.

66. Sometime parties in mediation, even though they lean toward cooperation, have tendencies to make negative attributions of each other. They often do this unconsciously, but the effects are destructive of good mediation outcomes. By leaning in to the language that the parties use — by calling attention to it in helpful ways — a good mediator can create awareness and perspective in the parties such that they might make different discursive choices as mediation progresses.

67. This raises the issue of skepticism about how much distortion we can actually overcome in the way we perceive things. On the other hand, I believe that through either a) dialogue with another or b) mediation, we can correct these distortions. Cooperative and empathetic discussion has an effective way of exposing distortions and also providing possibilities for new interpretations of self, other, and world that can lead to effective mediation consequences.

68. This view throws a wrench into the modern idea that we can be self aware and autonomous, instead arguing that we are playthings of the linguistic unconscious and are determined by it.

69. This theoretical clue about the self can motivate mediators to gently explore a client's perceived needs and preferences, knowing that the conscious mind may need additional reflection and dialogue in order to gain clarity and stability.

70. Promoting authentic and honest communication between the parties is an essential ingredient to successful mediation.

71. Successful mediation often involves parties who grow and evolve in their needs and preferences. It is an open question how much a party can grow in self awareness and into an evolved perspective about their selves and relational status post-resolution.

72. By infusing new language into the resolution process, a good

mediator can help open up new awareness and new possibilities for choice.

73. This is the heart and soul of good mediation: looking for creative possibilities.

74. Showing new language of cooperation can help anxious parties move away from competitive, adversarial language choices.

75. By looking at a person's current relationships we can understand the sum of his social intentionalities. This can give us valuable clues for how a party perceives the resolution possibilities of his current conflict.

76. In a future work that explores and develops more fully the application of phenomenology to mediation, I will consider Sartre's early construction of sado-masochistic dynamics, as well as his account of groups, especially a triad. This may shed some light on what happens in consciousness when a third person (mediator) interfaces with two disputing parties.

77. We can also imagine how frightened and anxious individuals can be when they dissolve a marriage or business structure. What might have formerly operated as ontological security is in the process of being lost, often without something or someone new to replace it. This leads to comments like "I don't know who I am anymore." In fact, the person saying this does not often know himself {his former self] anymore.

78. Ultimately this is the phenomenological approach.

Suggestions for Further Reading

Essays on Phenomenology and the Self, Kevin Boileau (EPIS Press, 2012)

Freud and Beyond, Stephen Mitchell (Basic Books, 1996)

Meditations on first Philosophy, Rene Descartes, trans. Donald Cress (Hackett, 1993)

The Routledge History of Philosophy (Routledge, 1993)

Mediation: Skills and Techniques, Michael Colatrella et al (Lexis Nexis, 2008)

The Critique of Pure Reason, Immanuel Kant (Cambridge University, 1999)

The Interpreted World, Ernesto Spinelli (Sage, 2005)

Relational Theory, Paul Wachtel (The Guilford Press, 2010)

Being and Nothingness, Jean-Paul Sartre (Washington Square Press, 1993)

Genuine Reciprocity and Group Authenticity, Kevin Boileau (EPIS Press, 2012)

Jacques-Lacan and the Philosophy of Psychoanalysis, Ellie Ragland-Sullivan (University of Illinois, 1987)

The Lacanian Subject, Bruce Fink (Princeton University, 1996)

Index

This book was written under the auspices and authority of the BCS Dispute Resolution Research Institute of North America. The institute has a number of research projects with the mission to lead to a deeper understanding of conflict and the different strategies humans use for resolution. Some of the major projects involve psychoanalysis, phenomenology, and the mathematics of game theory. The Institute also has an active mediation training program with beginning, intermediate, and advanced courses that are taught on ground and in webinar formats.

www.bcsmediationtraining.com

About EPIS Press

We established EPIS Press in the objective of publishing new work in the following areas of inquiry:

1) existential psychoanalysis & phenomenology;

2) traditional & contemporary psychoanalysis theoretical and clinical;

3) critical philosophy as it pertains to psychoanalysis, culture, phenomenology, and philosophy of mind;

4) new literature in phenomenology and psychoanalysis;

5) any related work as it bears on these issues, including neuropsychology and psychoanalysis.

For more information go to
EPIS Press
31 Fort Missoula Road
Suite 4
Missoula, MT 59804
epispublishing1@gmail.com
www.episworldwide.com